# MACY'S
## THANKSGIVING DAY PARADE

Dedicated to all of the Macy's employees who have given up their Thanksgiving Days during the past 75-plus years to give the nation the best present ever: the Macy's Thanksgiving Day Parade. (Courtesy of the *New York Daily News*.)

# MACY'S
## THANKSGIVING DAY PARADE

ARCADIA
PUBLISHING

Robert M. Grippo and Christopher Hoskins

Published by Arcadia Publishing
Charleston, South Carolina

Printed in the United States of America

Library of Congress Catalog Card Number: 2004101851

For all general information contact Arcadia Publishing at:
Telephone 843-853-2070
Fax 843-853-0044
E-mail sales@arcadiapublishing.com
For customer service and orders:
Toll-Free 1-888-313-2665

Visit us on the Internet at www.arcadiapublishing.com

*On the covers:* The front cover photograph appears courtesy of the Ballard Institute and Museum of Puppetry at the University of Connecticut. The back cover photograph appears courtesy of Lockheed Martin, Akron.

# CONTENTS

In a real coup, actor Edmund Gwenn rode in the 1946 parade as Santa Claus and even appeared at Macy's to make a speech. This resulted in some great footage for the 1947 film classic *Miracle on 34th Street*. The Baseball Player balloon is featured prominently in the film. Surprisingly, not one of the major newspapers made mention of Gwenn's appearance beforehand. According to the press the day after the parade, "A somewhat frostbitten Santa Claus, in the person of Edmund Gwenn the actor, gingerly climbed off his perch." (*Miracle on 34th Street,* copyright 1947 by Twentieth Century Fox. All rights reserved.)

The authors extend special thanks to the following for their tremendous generosity in providing images:

Ballard Institute and Museum of Puppetry, University of Connecticut
Goodyear Tire and Rubber Company
Lockheed Martin, Akron
Macy's Annual Events
*New York Daily News*
Bill Smith
20th Century Fox
University of Akron

# ACKNOWLEDGMENTS

When we began our journey through the history of the Macy's Thanksgiving Day Parade, we knew that we would meet and work with many people. We never thought, however, that we would meet so many special people. We are very proud to have had the chance to work with them and to be able to call them friends.

Our thanks go to Arcadia Publishing and our editor, Jennifer A. Durgin, and publisher, Tiffany Howe, for the faith and enthusiasm they put into our book to make it the celebration it is.

We are grateful to our agent, William Brown of QCorp, for taking our project and finding the right home at Arcadia Publishing.

At the *New York Daily News,* John Campi, Edward Fay, Eric Meskauskas, Griselda Garcia, Claus Guglberger, Bill Martin, Angela Troisi, and Lenore Schlossberg were extraordinarily gracious in making their extensive, historical, and glorious photograph archive available to us. (The archive can be viewed at www.dailynewspix.com.) We thank them for embracing our project with enthusiasm.

At the Goodyear Tire and Rubber Company in Akron, Ohio, Joan Reisig, Doc Pingree, and Phil Welch all generously shared their time and the history of Goodyear without hesitation.

At Lockheed Martin in Akron, Ohio, Cary Dell supplied us with rare images from the company's archives and gave us a tour of the landmark Goodyear Airdock in Akron, where many of the balloons from the 1930s were photographed. Some of those vintage photographs appear in the following pages.

We thank Frank Ballard of the the Ballard Institute and Museum of Puppetry at the University of Connecticut, who graciously invited us to walk through the museum of marionettes. He then put before us spectacular photographs that belonged to Tony Sarg, the man who invented the big balloons in 1927. We also extend our appreciation to Tamara Hunt, who led us in Frank Ballard's direction, and to Stephen J. Long, also of the Ballard Institute.

At the University of Akron, Dean Delmus Williams gave us full access to the Goodyear Tire and Rubber Company's archives. His assistance, along with John Miller's expertise as an archivist, helped us uncover many rare and exciting finds.

We also thank Joe Harris, the artist who gave life to Underdog. He shared our excitement in seeing each photograph and original blueprint of the classic Underdog balloon. He told us all the details of how Underdog became a Macy's Thanksgiving Day Parade balloon superstar that is fondly remembered to this day.

We thank Tiffany Ward, the keeper of Bullwinkle, one of her father Jay Ward's best-loved cartoon icons. She spent many hours with us discussing the original Bullwinkle balloon. She, too, shared the joy of seeing the balloon photographs and blueprints that we uncovered.

We thank fellow parade enthusiast and collector of rare parade photographs Bill Smith, who supplied many rare images that we are proud to say appear in this book for the first time anywhere.

We send our sincerest thanks to Andy Bandit and the staff at 20th Century Fox Film Corporation for graciously and wholeheartedly granting permission for use of the materials from the 1947 film classic *Miracle on 34th Street.* Thanks also go to Maureen O'Hara and her agent, Betty McCarth, for permission to use the photographs in which she appears. We are extremely proud and honored to include the images from that miracle of a film in this book.

We also thank these other friends of our book: Alex Drosin, Gary Hymowitz, Jean Free, Robert Thixton, Ben Moses, Larry Samele, and Milton DeLugg, who has been the musical director of the parade telecast since 1963. .

At Macy's, the parade is very special to everyone; each and every person speaks of it with joy. The caretakers of the parade love the work they do. They are truly wonderful people, and every year they present to the world a magical, wondrous gift: the Macy's Thanksgiving Day Parade. Bill Schermerhorn, Mark Schonberg (who, sadly, passed away in 2003), Ronnie Taffet, Martine Reardon, Diana Roio, Bob Rutan, Elina Kazan, and Rachelle Stern all gave us their support and trusted that we would take the love we had for the parade and put it down in words, creating a full history for all to read. Their assistance made this book a reality. Robin Hall has taken the lead from his predecessor, Jean McFaddin, and is continuing to make the parade a spectacular treat for children and the young at heart. We thank him for his support of our project. Manfred Bass, through words and images, shared a lifetime of his work in designing the floats and balloons that have brought miles of smiles to millions of parade fans. We thank him for sharing those memories with us and for working to turn his dreams into reality in the parade every year for nearly 40 years. Thanks go to John Piper, who, upon Manfred Bass's retirement, has continued to lead the Macy's Parade Studio to new heights of fun and fantasy, and to Robin Erichsen, also of the Macy's Parade Studio, for her A+ work.

We extend our thanks and love to Jean McFaddin. She opened her heart and the doors of Macy's to us when we approached her with our idea for the book. Without her, the parade would not have become the worldwide treasure it is and our book would never have been possible.

Last but not least, I am grateful to my mother for sitting me down in front of the television when I was just a tyke to watch the Macy's Thanksgiving Day Parade.

—Robert M. Grippo

# INTRODUCTION

# A PARADE LIKE
# NO OTHER

Each and every one of us has a favorite holiday. For some, nothing can beat Christmas Day or perhaps the Fourth of July. For me, my favorite holiday was and still is Thanksgiving Day. Thanksgiving is not only a day for family and friends to get together to give thanks for all their blessings but also a day for ushering in the holiday season with a celebration of floats, clowns, marching bands, celebrities, and, of course, balloons some 70 feet tall in the shape of cartoon characters of yesterday and today.

Thanksgiving Day in our house had its own ritual. We rose at the crack of dawn as Mom prepared the turkey for the anticipated meal, and then we took a choice position in the living room to watch the big event on television: the Macy's Thanksgiving Day Parade. As the heavenly aroma of the cooking turkey engulfed the house, we watched the giant Bullwinkle, Underdog, Mickey Mouse, Smokey the Bear, and Superman balloons as they cast shadows along the granite jungle. We were transfixed. Through the years, countless millions of people of all ages have lined the streets in rain, sleet, and snow to unite in one mass of holiday delight.

From its humble beginnings in 1924 through its present-day annual trek down the streets of Manhattan, the parade has entertained with a style all its own, a style different from any other parade. With its signature balloons and celebrity-decked floats, the parade has always welcomed the one and only Santa Claus to New York City. The history of the Macy's Thanksgiving Day Parade is rich with fantasy and dreamlike visions. Join us as we trace this treasured New York City tradition—which now, through television, is a national event—from its first line of march through its present-day high-stepping, show-stopping incarnation.

On Thanksgiving Day, November 27, 1924, the first march, led by police escort, started at 9:00 a.m. at 145th Street and Convent Avenue. Proceeding to Morningside Avenue and 110th Street, it traveled down Broadway to 34th Street, arriving at Macy's at noon for the unveiling of the Christmas windows entitled "The Fairy Frolics of Wondertown." Floats featuring the Old Lady in the Shoe, Little Miss Muffet, and Little Red Riding Hood thrilled the crowds lining the street, who enjoyed an impromptu circus featuring bears, elephants, and donkeys. Four bands gave the parade its merry music. That year's closing act became the parade's perennial finale: Santa Claus arriving in Herald Square to kick off the holiday season. Santa's sleigh arrived atop a mountain of ice. Sitting on his throne and sounding his trumpet, Santa gave the signal to unveil the Christmas windows. The crowd rushed to view Mother Goose characters portrayed as marionettes. The advertisements heralding a tremendous holiday tableau were not ballyhoo but fact. The press response was ecstatic. One journalist reported that the parade "was welcomed by such crowds," estimated at 10,000 in Herald Square, "that a large force of policemen had difficulty maintaining police lines." (Courtesy of Macy's.)

# One

# THE 1920S
## BANDS, CLOWNS,
## AND MERRYMAKERS

Surrounded by the sound of the wailing trumpet of Louis Armstrong, the flappers danced as the bootlegged whiskey flowed. Shortened skirts were the rage (and outrage), and Chicago mob boss Al Capone, with the help of the Tommy gun, showed the Windy City who was boss. Meanwhile, a quiet man named Calvin Coolidge, with money to burn, took the office of president. The Roaring Twenties were a decade with a sense of total abandonment. It was the Jazz Age, and life was good. The attitude that nothing could go wrong was shared by everyone. Despite Prohibition, in effect as of January 1920, spirits were high.

In 1924, R. H. Macy and Company, already part of the fabric of New York City, introduced two institutions: the first Seventh Avenue addition to the existing Broadway store in Herald Square (creating what became known as "the World's Largest Department Store") and the Macy's Christmas Parade. Yes, what we now know as Macy's Thanksgiving Day Parade started out as a Christmas pageant. R. H. Macy and Company was a company of immigrants, who were thankful for the opportunities that America and New York City gave them. They decided to give thanks and celebrate their good fortune with a tradition rooted in the festivals of their homelands: parades. Macy's employees incorporated their own traditions with what newspapers called an "Americanized modern slant." The press billed the event as "a surprise New York will never forget."

Preceding the 1925 parade, Macy's sponsored an amateur photograph contest with $500 in prizes to be awarded. Judges included staff from major New York newspapers—some of which are now just a memory, including the *New York Herald Tribune.* One judge, noted puppeteer and theatrical designer Tony Sarg, was also responsible for Macy's holiday windows and for staging the parade.

By 1926, some 300 Macy's employees were involved in staging the event, which was scheduled between 1:00 p.m. and 4:00 p.m. so that spectators could go to their houses of worship as decreed by Pres. Calvin Coolidge.

With the fourth annual Macy's Christmas Parade ready for its march, Macy's president, Jesse L. Strauss, announced at a luncheon on Tuesday, November 22, 1927, that the event would be "bigger and better than ever." His statement could not have been more prophetic, for that year marked the first appearance of what would become the parade's superstars and goodwill ambassadors: the giant character balloons.

Again, Tony Sarg had designed the parade and Christmas windows. According to press coverage, Sarg "spoke wistfully, of sixty-foot dinosaurs and twenty-five foot dachshunds which will be in the line of march." The parade was to start "after a fence has been torn down to permit its egress from a vacant lot where it is to form at 110th St." Starting time was set at 1:00 p.m. The lion's share of the press coverage was devoted to the premiere of the giant balloons. The press noted, "Following the police vanguard of the pageant was a human behemoth," a balloon 21 feet tall. Much was made of the fact that this human greeted spectators at second-story windows along the route. Because of its height, the balloon had to be lowered so it could "crawl" under the elevated train line at 66th Street and Broadway.

The show-stopping figure of the parade was the 60-foot dinosaur, which was escorted by a tribe of cavemen. The 25-foot dachshund (not a balloon, but a papier mâché costume needing two people to bring it to life) was accompanied by turkeys, chickens, and ducks of heroic size. Although the balloons were the main attraction, the crowd also enjoyed nine floats, featuring, among others, Robinson Crusoe, Little Red Riding Hood and the Wolf, a yule log drawn by woodsmen, and a puppet show animated by "twelve of the prettiest girls employed at Macy's," according to the press. Providing music were bands of the 71st Regiment, the 103rd Infantry, and the 22nd Engineers.

The 1928 parade commenced at 2:30 p.m. Led by the 71st Regiment band, clowns, doing what came naturally, clowned around balloons in the shape of a 40-foot-long blue elephant, a 60-foot-long tiger, and a 50-foot hummingbird. Macy's brought fantasy to life. At the end of the parade, Tony Sarg directed the release of five inflatables that were timed with slow leaks to stay aloft for approximately a week. Macy's issued a reward of $100 each for their return. Escorted by snowmen, Santa Claus rode into Herald Square on a housetop float, its chimney loaded with toys. As an estimated 100,000 children watched, enraptured, jolly St. Nick climbed the Macy's marquee to direct the unveiling of the Christmas windows, which were entitled "The Exploits of Columbus" and featured animated marionettes.

All was in readiness for the parade to get under way at 1:00 p.m. on Thursday, November 28, 1929. By that time, Macy's was choosing famous cartoon characters to become giant balloons. The main attractions were larger-than-life inflatables of the Katzenjammer family, characters from a famous comic strip of the era that featured the mischievous shenanigans of the Katzenjammer kids, Hans and Fritz, and the captain, who tried in vain to bring order to the household.

With 10 balloons being released, an increase from the five released the previous year, Macy's kept the total reward amount at $500 by offering $50 apiece for the balloons' return. Suburbanites located in the vicinity of Roosevelt Field on Long Island were given the heads-up, as newspapers noted that prevailing winds had sent the balloons in their direction.

On Wednesday, November 26, 1930, colorful blurbs appeared in newspapers previewing the next day's events. November 27, 1930, was a brisk day, and snow flurries were in the air (the first time snow fell on the event, but not the last), which gave spectators a Currier and Ives helping of holiday cheer. The event was scheduled to begin at 110th Street and Amsterdam Avenue. That year, 15 comic character balloons were released in front of Macy's. As each balloon was released, shouts from the crowds were heard from blocks away. The balloons danced and swayed in the breeze, taking on a life of their own. The concrete buildings of the city were hidden behind a rush of smaller colorful balloons, adding to the merriment. Music for the event was supplied by the bands of the 71st Regiment, the 9th Coast Artillery, and the 102nd Engineers. Wrapping up the event, Tony Sarg broadcast a message over the radio advising residents of the Eastern seaboard to watch the skies, as the balloons might be heading their way.

As the 1920s came to a close, it was clear the parade had been a major success. Originally envisioned as a thank-you from a group of Macy's employees and proudly sponsored by the biggest department store in the world, the parade became a cherished event unique to New York City. New Yorkers took the event to heart, and for a couple of hours on Thanksgiving Day, even the most cynical became believers in fantasy. After beginning as a kind of circus parade chock-full of ragamuffins (a term used to describe the clowns and various other merrymakers), it began to take shape as a truly wondrous and magical Macy's miracle.

With the addition of the larger-than-life, helium-inflated heroes, the signature that distinguished this parade was established. Given all the hoopla surrounding each of the first seven editions, could anything else add to the spectacle known as the Macy's Christmas Parade? Concerns arose, however, as the mood of the country took a turn for the worse with the October 1929 stock market crash. Dark and lean times lay ahead. Would the parade continue to uplift the masses and bring joy to all, even if only for a few hours?

It was official: the Macy's proclamation appearing in newspapers the day after Thanksgiving 1924 stated that the parade would return on November 26, 1925. The 1925 parade was bigger that the first one, delivering a spectacle of five bands. Fantastic sights included a 100-foot caterpillar snaking down the city streets, cages of animals from the Central Park Zoo, and an elephant that reportedly said "papa." Again, Santa Claus was the crowd pleaser, riding a gigantic globe that rested on huge icebergs and was driven by a team of polar bears (horses). Stepping down to take residence on his glittering throne of gold, Santa was proclaimed "King of All the Children of Greater New York." Macy's Long Island City warehouse was forced into service, accommodating the construction of bigger and more elaborate floats, which were assembled overnight at 110th Street. (Courtesy of Macy's.)

At the 1926 parade, a crowd estimated at 10,000 viewed what was promised as a "Charming Cinderella and her Radiant Retinue," as well as Merry Bumpkins and the Impossible Looking Clowns and an airplane suspended by a huge derrick. Santa's entrance was followed by Tony Sarg's elaborate marionette window show entitled "The A-B-C Antics." (Courtesy of Macy's.)

13

The top cartoon star of the day, Felix the Cat, appeared in balloon form in 1927. (Courtesy of Bill Smith collection.)

In the early photographs of these first larger-than-life inflatables, such as this 1927 image of Felix the Cat, the characters look crude but possess a certain charm. Later, Macy's began doing the balloons in-house, and their quality continues to improve, resulting in spectacular, eye-popping representations of our most beloved cartoon characters. (Courtesy of Bill Smith collection.)

to-day!

macy's
fifth annual
christmas
parade
weather permitting

through the heart of new york
down broadway, 110th st. to 34th st.
1 to 3 pm

**This Humming Bird is a Hummer. She's tuning up for Macy's Christmas Parade today**

'Mid roar of brass and beaten drums
The gay parade—see, here it comes!
Children screaming with delight
Laughter, Splendor—What a sight!

Clowns in antics rare and gay;
You've never seen them act that way.
Monster floats and living toys
AND Santa Claus—Oh, Joy of Joys!

Animals who grunt and roar
Their like has ne'er been seen before.
Come, if you want some stirring fun,
See Macy's Big Parade at One,

For line of March and
details of rewards see page 21

**MACY'S**
34TH ST. AND BROADWAY

Press coverage of the 1928 parade focused on another related tradition: procuring a choice location along the parade route. Parents stood by their children on the curbs. For many New Yorkers, the parade was becoming an event that fathers took their anxious children to while mothers prepared the turkey. (Courtesy of Macy's.)

15

Two mishaps occurred in 1928 that were given press coverage. The press reported, "Near Ninetieth Street the giant dog balloon grew restive and tore loose from his leash held by members of Macy's packing and receiving departments." And at 58th Street and Sixth Avenue, the wind blew the great inflated turkey against a No Parking sign. Deflated, the two balloons were removed from the parade. This photograph from 1929 shows the repaired turkey and Mrs. Katzenjammer. (Courtesy of Bill Smith collection.)

The balloon release of 1928 was a spectacle worthy of a Jules Verne novel. As noted in the press the day after the parade, "The largest crowd to witness a balloon ascension in this city for many years, stood open-mouthed on the pavement of Thirty-fourth Street, in front of the R. H. Macy store." (Courtesy of Bill Smith collection.)

Reports mentioned the fun in handling the balloons, as each close call and near miss was cheered by the crowds. Coverage was given almost exclusively to the balloon mishaps for the sixth edition of the parade in 1929. Some difficulty was experienced by the balloon Herr-Inspector, which traveled without altitude (explaining his attitude). "An air thermometer hovering around the freezing point was not to his liking," the press said. "He would not go up, even an extra shot of helium failed to put the spirit in him." Helium, the magic elixir, was held ready for such emergencies. Note that his whiskers were cut to give him lift. One of the Katzenjammer Kids, in a mischievous mood, headed for the new Empire State Building and was then seen to rise to the 70th floor, lean over, and look down at the masses. Unfortunately, the figure got caught in a fierce wind that carried it over the East River, where it was obscured by falling snow. (Courtesy of Goodyear Tire and Rubber Company collection, University of Akron Archives.)

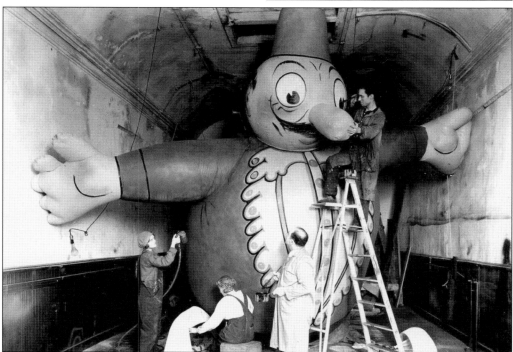

Press coverage became more detailed as each fantastic float, tableau, or balloon took its place in the line of march. Seen here in 1929, Tony Sarg (center) and puppeteer Bil Baird (right) touch up the Terrible Turk, who fits the bill. Baird later became a famous puppeteer. (Courtesy of Bill Smith collection.)

This 1930 newspaper advertisement heralds the parade. (Courtesy of Macy's.)

After the 1930 parade, crowds rush to see the Macy's Christmas windows. (Courtesy of Ballard Institute of Puppetry, University of Connecticut.)

Aided by the wind, all the balloons rose swiftly after the 1930 parade. The balloons were again fixed with slow leaks, allowing them to stay aloft for up to one week. The balloons held the reward information in a waterproof envelope. Noting the snowfall, Santa proclaimed, "I seemed to have brought down a blizzard with me." His dirigible, which had the inscription "A Happy Christmas," was then released to join the other larger-than-life balloons high above the streets of the big city. (Courtesy of Ballard Institute of Puppetry, University of Connecticut.)

In 1930, Santa Claus arrived in his dirigible, which he then exited, heading for Macy's canopy on 34th Street. After a fanfare of trumpets, Santa sat on his red-cushioned, gilded throne, blowing kisses to the estimated 25,000 children and adults enjoying the spectacle in Herald Square. He then gave the signal to begin a marionette holiday extravaganza. (Courtesy of Ballard Institute of Puppetry, University of Connecticut.)

The balloons were the stars of the parade in 1931. An enormously inflated Felix the Cat made the quickest ascension. He headed toward the Empire State Building, clearing with room to spare. (Courtesy of Ballard Institute of Puppetry, University of Connecticut.)

Felix Jr., the little shaver, still needed four men to hold him down. He is seen here in 1931. (Courtesy of Bill Smith collection.)

In preparation for the 1933 parade, the smaller balloons were inflated in Newark and trucked into New York; the larger ones were inflated at 110th Street with plenty of time to spare. Balloons such as Jerry the Pig, Felix the Cat, Fritz the Dachshund, and the Colicky Kid (pictured here) made it down the route unscathed. (Courtesy of *New York Daily News.*)

# Two

# The 1930s
## The Mouse Follows
## the Cat

As the Depression tightened its grip on the nation, bread lines stretched for blocks and soup kitchens served needy folk whose life dreams had been shattered. Politicians promised better times ahead. Common headlines like "Mayor Promises 200,000 Jobs" offered some hope to the unemployed. Thankfully, Pres. Franklin D. Roosevelt presented the New Deal; but was it hype or hope? Meanwhile, the major form of entertainment was the movies. For 5¢ to 75¢, gorgeous theater palaces gave desperate audiences hope, offering everything from upbeat, peppy musicals to rat-a-tat-tat gangster epics. Rising stars, such as Clark Gable, Jean Harlow, and a little curly-topped bundle of pep named Shirley Temple, made the nation forget its troubles.

Just as the tide seemed to be turning and promises of prosperity seemed close to being realized, war clouds began to gather ominously. By the end of the decade, there were serious thoughts of possible involvement by the United States in what would become a world war. Through it all, the country still gave thanks, and to help lift a city and its people, the parade marched on. It was clear everyone loved a parade—a parade that was soon rechristened the Macy's Thanksgiving Day Parade. In these hard times, holiday cheer was Macy's gift to the people of New York City.

On November 26, 1931, at 1:30 p.m., with the leading band playing "Roll On, You Mississippi, Roll On," the eighth edition of Macy's Christmas Parade marched ahead. Right behind a 20-foot caterpillar, the Terrible Turk, his ferocious sneer failing to menace the crowd, kept the procession moving toward Macy's in Herald Square. The parade met its promised length of 15 blocks.

All went well, and the event was a smashing success. But there was still a bit of highflying drama to come. A transoceanic pilot, Col. Clarence D. Chamberlin, was navigating his plane over Brooklyn after departing from Floyd Bennett Field with a load of sightseers when he spotted a curious object: Felix the Cat, who was enjoying his freedom and taking in the sights himself. (One newspaper claimed it was the Blue Hippopotamus, but indeed it was Felix.) Chamberlin had no intention of tangling with the mighty cat until one of the passengers suggested he grab it in midair. Although he was a flier with vast experience, Chamberlin was unsure of the procedures for such matters. After maneuvering the plane alongside the balloon, he nabbed the beast over Jamaica Bay with one of the plane's wings and headed back to the field, carrying Felix to safety. Chamberlin reported seeing several other balloons settling over Jamaica Bay. At press time, he reportedly was still unsure whether to return the balloon or add it to his other trophies.

The parade had entered the 1930s in a smashing, eye-popping, and unexpectedly dramatic fashion. But the following year's edition was to be even more dramatic and harrowing. The events of Thanksgiving Day 1932 had a lasting effect on the handling of the big balloons. A less-than-spectacular advertisement preceded the parade, but all of the important tidbits were dispensed in an efficient manner: "Santa Claus will proceed from there down Broadway on a giant locomotive, with bands, balloons, clowns, floats, and colossal helium filled animals in his wake." After the plane-grabbing of Felix the year before, Macy's still released the balloons but issued a warning to other fliers via the newspapers that no prizes would be given to aviators who downed the balloons.

The ninth annual edition kicked off in fine form on November 24, 1932. A parade veteran, the 60-foot-long Tom-Cat, led the procession; next came the locomotive that was bestowed with the honor of carrying Santa Claus into Herald Square. Noah's Ark was escorted by four Macy's clerks dressed as rabbits. Back in the line of march, a skittish Felix was no doubt hoping to avoid another run-in with Chamberlin. The largest balloon, Andy the Alligator, measured 150 feet long; this gator could not have been greater.

For all the suspense, nothing could prepare the people of New York City for what happened next. The parade had ended with the usual release of the giant balloons, with a reward offered for their return. At approximately 4:00 p.m., Annette Gibson, a 22-year-old resident of Prospect Place, and her flying instructor, Hugh Copeland, a resident of Woodside, Queens, were flying over Jamaica, New York, in a biplane. After reportedly gliding down to 5,000 feet and then leveling off, Gibson spotted one of the behemoth balloons—what she thought was a yellow and red dragon—coming into view. Upon closer inspection, it turned out to be the Tom-Cat balloon. She shouted, "I think I'll have a piece of the neck," to Copeland, as she took dead aim on the cat. Upon impact, the balloon wrapped itself around the left wing. The plane went into a deep tailspin and sped toward the ground out of control. In an effort to prevent a fire upon impact, Gibson shut off the ignition. Witnesses in the surrounding neighborhoods, straining their necks to look skyward, gasped as they heard the engine die and saw the plane plummeting to earth. Copeland quickly pushed Gibson out of the way and tried to get control of the craft. As Gibson fell into the front seat, the cabin door flew open, and the only thing that came between her and a quick exit from the plane was the safety belt that caught her foot.

The first thing Copeland did was switch the plane's ignition back on. Thankfully, the engine sputtered on immediately. As the plane came within 80 feet of the rooftops of Queens, Copeland lifted it to safety. After heading back to the airfield at Roosevelt Field, Gibson shrugged off the close brush with death, but she reportedly commented, "I have something to be thankful for this Thanksgiving."

With two plane incidents within two years, R. H. Macy's made the decision to no longer release the balloons at the end of the parade. The excitement was not lessened, however, as the parade was excitement itself from the very first march. Even today, reports from newspapers indicate that most police officers on duty for the parade are volunteers; they regard the parade as a special event. In the past, a mounted police unit escorted Macy's officials along the route, heading the march. Today, a police motorcycle unit escorts parade officials into Herald Square. Macy's and the people of New York City regard the police escorts with the honor they so rightly deserve.

The estimated one million people (one-seventh of the city's population at the time) who lined the parade route for the 10th edition were in for a treat on November 30, 1933, as Macy's put on another great parade. In 1934, Santa Claus again rode on the last float, which was described as regal. The float was drawn by six Horace Horsecollars, a Walt Disney star. The first balloon version of Mickey Mouse appeared in the parade this year, and celebrity Eddie Cantor welcomed Santa Claus at the Macy's marquee. The windows of the store, which depicted scenes from the poem "'Twas the Night Before Christmas," were unveiled upon Santa's arrival. A total of 200 white balloons were released at the wave of Santa's hand, with cash prize certificates awaiting their return. Witnesses reported that the balloons were heading in the direction of New Jersey. With the custom of releasing the giant balloons now stopped and the addition of celebrities to the celebration (film star Eddie Cantor appeared at Macy's after the 1934 parade passed by), the parade was being shaped into the event we know today.

November 28, 1935, was a cloudy, rain-threatened day. The downpour held off until the parade reached 34th Street for the scheduled finale. Then the skies opened up, sending spectators in a frantic search for shelter. Even the flash rainstorm did not drown the spirits that had been lifted by the sights of the 12th annual march. Nine bands provided musical accompaniment to the masses awaiting Santa Claus. When the parade passed in front of Macy's, Paul Whiteman provided a taste of holiday cheer, conducting the assembled bands in "Adeste Fideles" as the Christmas-decked windows were unveiled.

On November 25, 1937, the parade was advertised to take a new route, starting at 110th Street and heading to Amsterdam Avenue, Central Park West, south to Columbus Circle, and finally to 34th Street. The parade started at 1:00 p.m. and was due to arrive at Macy's around 3:00 p.m.

The ceremonies at Macy's were covered by WOR radio's Uncle Don, popular bandleader Benny Goodman (then appearing at the Hotel Pennsylvania), and radio singer Jessica Dragonette, best remembered as the singing voice of the princess in the 1939 Max Fleischer–produced animated feature *Gulliver's Travels*. At Macy's, Santa dedicated the store windows, which featured a "World's Fair of Toys" (already preparing New Yorkers for the upcoming 1939 World's Fair) and a Midway of Marvels, to the boys and girls of New York.

In the 1937 parade, Pinocchio's identity was confirmed by his 44-foot-long or 68-foot-long nose (newspaper reports of its length varied). His escorts consisted of men in harlequin costumes all sporting exaggerated proboscises. At the 1938 parade, floats drew considerable applause, being almost as popular as the inflatables. Fishermen surrounded a whale float, designed by a schoolboy from Brooklyn. One of the fishermen brandished a toy harpoon, which he lunged as if to catch a mighty whale. Another popular tableau included Rip Van Winkle, who celebrated the event by drinking from his flagon. Other fabulous tales were brought to life in fantastic form, including Sinbad and his Roc, Snow White and the Seven Dwarfs, and Old Mother Hubbard. One float depicted the anticipated event of the upcoming year: the 1939 New York World's Fair, to be held in Flushing Meadows.

Though pelted by hail, the spectators enjoyed the holiday cheer. A parade of clowns and their sidesplitting antics, uniformed soldiers marching uniformly, and knights gallantly riding their steeds with armor shining in its medieval splendor ushered two hours of cheer into Herald Square. The man of the hour, Santa Claus, rode on a float representing snow-covered housetops; it still is one of the most memorable floats to ever be in the parade. Bringing to life the vision of Santa's Christmas Eve trip, which had only been described in the written word, this incarnation presented, with just the right touch of magic, the now-classic tableau dreamt of by children for generations. Waiting to greet Santa at Macy's was big-band leader Kay Kyser from the Kollege of Musical Knowledge.

The year 1939 marked the release of *The Wizard of Oz,* and Macy's had a gigantic Tin Man balloon, followed by the Wicked Witch (a small float), of course. Santa also had the honor of being "balloonified" (at 57 feet tall) that year. Streamlined Ford tractors pulled a total of 16 floats, and for the first time, there were no horse-drawn floats in the parade. An advertisement made note of the "fleet of helium-filled Sarg designed side-splitting balloons—your sides—not theirs, we hope!" and "the unveiling of the holiday windows designed by illustrator Russell Patterson." (Patterson designed the windows, but Sarg was still designing the balloons, as noted.) Also advertised proudly was the fact that the parade would be televised: "The First Thanksgiving Day Parade to be TELEVISED. NBC will put it on the short waves from 12 Noon to 1PM." Televisions of the time were primitive, featuring very small screens; the television boom was delayed due to the onset of World War II.

The television "apparatus," as the camera was called, was placed at Central Park West just above the Museum of Natural History so that "sit-at-homers" could view the event in "cushioned ease." Police officers numbered 2,500, and they were there to maintain order and, like the crowds, to have a good time. The parade commenced in what was described as the best weather in the parade's history. The day was mild and sunny, which gave the one million spectators plenty to be thankful for, especially in light of the rain and sleet that accompanied the parades during the years of the Great Depression.

Returning that year were the Pinocchio balloon and the Big Man, Little Man balloon. Veterans of previous marches, the balloons were welcomed by the crowds. Popeye the Sailor joined the parade on a float this year, navigating his boat down the sometimes treacherous sea of city streets. From his view on the bridge of his vessel, rocked by mechanical waves, he greeted the kids, and they responded wildly. In a poll taken in 1938, Popeye was the most popular cartoon character, even more popular than Mickey Mouse.

Waiting on a reviewing stand for the arrival of Santa and the Snow Queen, who had tin soldiers as escorts along the route, were bandleader Eddie Duchin and his singer Jane Pickens performing "The Star Spangled Banner." Upon arriving at Macy's, Santa presided over the ceremonies to unveil the huge Macy's storefront windows, which included a toy land with 26 miniature floats on a revolving belt. Other wonders included the tableau entitled "The Wedding of the Wooden Soldier and the Painted Doll." The parade was again a crowd pleaser.

On Thursday, November 21, 1940, movie star Eddie Cantor was scheduled to greet Santa at Macy's again. Santa, arriving on a float depicting his Christmas Eve sleigh ride over the rooftops, snapped his whip and urged his team of reindeer to go faster as he sent greetings to the crowd over a microphone. The parade had weathered almost every type of climate during the preceding decade and had come through in highflying fashion. Every year, close to a million people had been thrilled by the holiday spectacle.

In the 1931 parade were three bands and a calliope. Crowds were estimated at 300,000 along the route, with 100,000 estimated in both Times Square and Herald Square. Making the day sweeter still, 45,000 lollipops were handed out to the youngsters lining the route. People stood on top of cars, and parents held children on their shoulders (and even on the reporters' shoulders), cheering the appearance of George the Giant Drum Major (pictured) and the Blue Hippopotamus. The mishap of note involved the Terrible Turk, who had a run-in with an electric sign at 72nd Street and broke in half. It seemed that, even at 40 feet tall, he was not as terrible as he looked. Inflatable delights included a two-headed man decked out in yellow trousers and black cavalry boots, who was fittingly described by the press as having an "impolite habit of peering into fourth story windows on both sides of the street." (Courtesy of Bill Smith collection.)

At the end of the 1931 parade, each balloon was escorted to 34th Street between Seventh and Sixth Avenues, where the balloons were given a shot of helium in an attempt to help them clear the crowds and skyscrapers as they headed for the heavens. Filled to capacity, the Blue Hippopotamus was the first to go, gaining altitude rapidly after a slow start and making a beeline toward Brooklyn after a brush with the Empire State Building. (Courtesy of Ballard Institute of Puppetry, University of Connecticut.)

Tiamat the Dragon, a red-and-yellow, 170-foot-long monster, had difficulty keeping his tail from hitting buildings along the route in 1931. Tiamat was the last to float away, heading toward Governor's Island. (Courtesy of *New York Daily News*.)

Jerry the Pig delights the crowd in 1932. (Courtesy of Bill Smith collection.)

"Lions and tigers and bears, oh my!" The balloons are almost ready in 1932. (Courtesy of Bill Smith collection.)

Reddy Red Bird flies high above the streets of New York City in this 1932 view. In 1933, to accommodate the crowds and traffic, Broadway was closed off between 110th Street and Columbus Avenue. That year, winds tore Andy the Alligator in two, causing the reptile to lose his tail just south of 70th Street. Andy was described as a "mildewed cucumber" and was reported to be "heading in the general direction of London, England." (Courtesy of Bill Smith collection.)

In 1932, the balloon that made the quickest exit upon its release was Tom-Cat, who cleared the Empire State Building in an estimated four minutes. Besides the onlookers lining the length of the route, scores more could be seen peering out of windows from the buildings on Broadway. Their view was second only to that of the giant balloons themselves. (Courtesy of Ballard Institute of Puppetry, University of Connecticut.)

The crowd at the 1932 parade agrees: this is one fine feline. (Courtesy of Goodyear Tire and Rubber Company collection, University of Akron Archives.)

Tony Sarg, seen here in 1933, seems to be saying, "There's got to be a better way of inflating these balloons." (Courtesy of Bill Smith collection.)

# !! HERE COMES THE PARADE !!

## IT'S IMMENSE! IT'S COLOSSAL! COME A-RUNNING!!

**THE TIME?** Today. Thanksgiving Day. 2:00 o'clock sharp it starts. Rain or shine. Don't be late! At approximately 4:30 Santa Claus will unveil Macy's Christmas Toy windows.

**THE PLACE?** Straight down Broadway from 110th Street to 34th. Miles of fun and frolic. Fabulous floats ...booming bands ...capering clowns... it's a riot ...bring the kids!

▼▼▼▼▼▼▼▼▼▼▼▼▼▼▼▼▼

**SEE THEM! HEAR THEM! TONY SARG'S**

## Helium Filled Monsters

### ! ! ! ! ! ! ! !

He laughs like a thousand men!

## GULLIVER THE GULLIBLE

He peeps in eighth story windows ... believes what he sees ... and laughs while he looks. Takes 40 men to hold him. The Greatest Gas Bag in History!

Oink! Oink! Here Comes

## JERRY THE PIG

Grunting and squealing. You can hear him from the Battery to the Bronx! He's 30 feet from snout to curly cue.

**HE WRIGGLES! HE WRITHES!**

## Andy the Alligator

He's agile. He's articulate. He hisses and he sizzles. 90 feet of lashing, slashing reptile!

Listen to him SQUALL!!

## THE COLICKY KID

He's mad. He's bad. He yowls bloody murder!

## And that's not All! SEE

JUMBO AND JOCKO ... FELIX THE CAT AND HIS 2-LEGGED KITTEN!
A MOOSE A DINO-SAUR A HUGE DUCK
A MONSTER ROOSTER and a GI-GAN-TIC HIPPO!

### Clowns! Clowns! Clowns!

Balloons! 10,000 Balloons!

AND LAST BUT NOT LEAST

# SANTA CLAUS (HIMSELF IN PERSON)
## In a Dog Sled Drawn by 11 Huskies to
# MACY'S

**MACY'S WILL BE CLOSED ALL DAY TODAY (THANKSGIVING DAY)**

Photograph taken in the airships Messr's Akron hangar.

In 1933, despite the advertised 11 huskies, Santa and his sled (a truck disguised as a sled) were led into Herald Square by only 8 dogs. Times being what they were, Santa was more than happy to sacrifice. Once again enthroned on Macy's marquee, he gave a speech that was broadcast over WOR radio in New York City, signaling the release of 5,000 multicolored balloons. In a new twist, 200 red-starred balloons, each three feet in diameter, were released as well. Upon retrieval, these treasured balloons fetched valued prizes: merchandise from Macy's. Musical veterans of the parade, the 71st Regiment and the 102nd Engineers, kept the parade in tune, accompanied by trucks providing amplification so paradegoers would not miss the cheerful holiday music. With mainstays such as clowns, marchers, and the like, the parade was fresh and exciting. (Courtesy of Macy's.)

Stiff westerly winds at cross streets could have wreaked havoc at the 1933 parade if not for the adept balloon handlers (like the ones handling big puppy Fritz the Dachshund) who had a number of years' experience behind them. (Courtesy of Goodyear Tire and Rubber Company collection, University of Akron Archives.)

Leading the line of march in 1933 was the five-story-tall Gulliver, seen here in the airdock at Akron, Ohio. Gulliver needed a repair after his nose was punctured. At Lincoln Square, he was given a quick repair and more helium; by the time he reached 47th Street, he was in fine form. (Courtesy of Ballard Institute of Puppetry, University of Connecticut.)

This is an advertisement for the 1934 parade. One of the keys to the parade's success was Macy's choice of characters to be made into balloons. Celebrities also added excitement. In 1934, legendary entertainer Eddie Cantor appeared in person at Macy's for the parade's finale. Cantor had been making a string of very entertaining and profitable films under contract to Samuel Goldwyn. In fact, one of his best films, *Kid Millions,* was in release in 1934. Cantor was also portrayed by a 50-foot-tall, helium-filled version of himself. In 1935, Harpo Marx became the only other person known to have been portrayed by a Macy's balloon. (Courtesy of Macy's.)

To this day, Macy's possesses an uncanny ability to pick just the right cartoon character to tickle the fancy of young and old alike. By 1934, the most popular cartoon character—in fact a bona fide superstar, known the world over—was Walt Disney's Mickey Mouse. (Courtesy of Bill Smith collection.)

In a savvy move, Macy's teamed for the first time with Disney for the 11th march in 1934. The collaboration, which continues today, provided for balloon versions of Disney's celebrated characters. Cartoon characters that usually graced Disney's *Silly Symphonies* seemed to leap from the silver screen and frolic along the parade route, to the delight of children and their parents. (Courtesy of Bill Smith collection.)

With nearly 2,000 police officers in attendance in 1934, all went well. The mounted police escorts were followed by a squadron of clowns bearing signs that spelled out "Hail Santa—Merry Christmas." These holiday revelers were followed by a marching band, and then came Mickey Mouse, all 40 feet of him. (Courtesy of *New York Daily News*.)

In 1935, Mickey Mouse was the biggest cartoon celebrity of the day and a star balloon, too. (Courtesy of Bill Smith collection.)

Despite intermittent drizzle, a crowd estimated at 500,000 and described by the press as "two solid walls" of people lined the route of the 1935 parade from the usual starting point at 110th Street. The true parade fans—those with an umbrella and those without, who stood in doorways or under anything that afforded dry space—waited an estimated 25 minutes for the big parade to pass by, their spirits undampened by the inclement weather. The press hammed up the portly Little Pig balloon's difficulty at the elevated train line at 65th Street and again at 53rd Street. Canvas was quickly placed on the street to protect the pig from the rough pavement. He was slowly glided under the structures on his back to successfully rise again and finish his parade trek. Following up the rear in hopeful pursuit was the Big Bad Wolf, pictured above, who was right at home in the canyon of city buildings. No matter how hard he huffed and puffed, he could never topple them. (Courtesy of Goodyear Tire and Rubber Company collection, University of Akron Archives.)

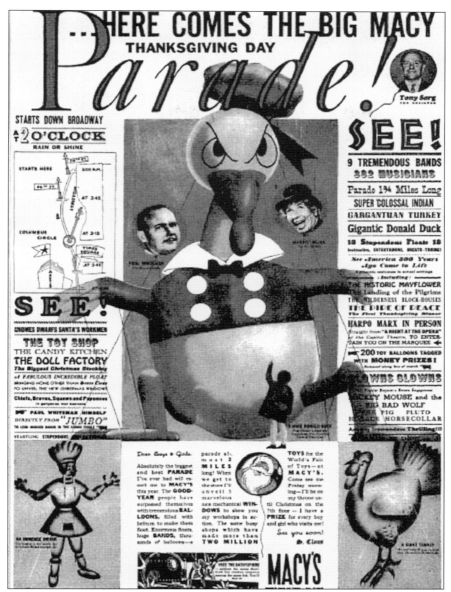

After being called Macy's Christmas Parade since its first march (with the exception of the 1934 Macy's Santa Claus Parade), the parade underwent a name change. The print advertisements that appeared in such papers as the *Daily News* on Wednesday, November 27, 1935, proclaimed, "Here Comes the Big Macy Thanksgiving Day Parade!" The star balloon debuting this year was Walt Disney's Donald Duck. This balloon was one of the first inflatables that could be classified as spectacular, featuring a fairly close resemblance to Donald's cartoon appearance. Of course, one must check out Donald's films of the era. He does look different than the wise-quacking duck that has been relatively unchanged in design since the 1940s. As the parade continued, the balloons became even more detailed, with some truly memorable highflying, helium-filled wonders. Balloons returning that year were Mickey Mouse, Horace Horsecollar, the Big Bad Wolf, and Pluto. The Tony Sarg–designed, 1.75-mile parade put smiles on the faces of young and old. (Courtesy of Macy's.)

Although Donald Duck received quite a bit of attention in 1935, the real star of the show was the big Indian. Newspapers noted, "The Indian was billed by the advance agent as *super colossal,* and he was. . . . His fierce painted eyes stared into fifth-story apartment windows and hotel windows, while his feet hit Broadway's high spots." Macy's chief Indian "was given, at moments, to a peculiar tribal dance to which his body swayed from side to side." With just the right combination of wind and balloon handling, his huge hands reached down to touch the heads of children and adults, resulting in shouts of glee. Most of the 18 floats presented historical tableaux, including the advertised Mayflower and Pilgrim presentation. The Mayflower, with yellow masts and red trim, was followed by a Plymouth Rock float, drawn by two white horses, with a group of early settlers perched upon it, ready to set foot in the New World. Next, a group of Pilgrims on a snow-covered house float was followed by another group eating the first Thanksgiving dinner. (Courtesy of Bill Smith collection.)

At the 1936 parade, the only balloon mishap happened to Father Knickerbocker, a glorious and richly detailed figure who got his nose stuck in the elevated train line at Lincoln Square. "Emergency crews rushed up, did a bit of plastic surgery on old Diedrich's nose, pumped his head full and he started south again," reported the press. In the early balloon years, Macy's had a sort of deflation doctor crew, specializing in rubber (not plastic) surgery, that rushed to the aid of the injured balloon to perform a quick repair job. Helium was pumped into the balloon, enabling it to continue its stroll down the streets of the city. It took 35 handlers to keep Father Knickerbocker on his path—not an easy task for the Colonial-garbed entourage. Through all of this, "Old Knick" kept his smile as he greeted spectators in seventh- and eighth-story windows along the streets. Dressed to the nines in a huge hat and a Colonial-style long coat decorated with a double column of buttons, he saluted each and every person with his right hand held high. (Courtesy of *New York Daily News*.)

Balloon inflation began in the morning on parade day in 1936, and the behemoths, especially the 120-foot Nantucket Sea Monster, took a good amount of time to reach flying size. The dragon had to pass under an elevated train track on its side, a maneuver the handlers accomplished deftly, to the cheers of the onlookers. The procession was led by the mounted police, followed by six armor-encased knights atop yellow-plumed horses. (Courtesy of Goodyear Tire and Rubber Company collection, University of Akron Archives.)

The second two-headed balloon to appear in the parade is seen here in 1936. (Courtesy of Bill Smith collection.)

At 43 feet tall, a balloon advertised as the world's largest Christmas stocking needed 23 gnomelike handlers with white beards to guide it to Macy's in the 1937 parade. A float singled out as memorable by the crowds and the press that year was Gulliver Captured by the Lilliputians. For the first time in a Macy's parade, a bagpipe band joined the line of march. Bringing up the rear again was Santa Claus atop a float featuring reindeer and the toys that the jolly man was to distribute to eagerly awaiting children the world over. (Courtesy of Goodyear Tire and Rubber Company collection, University of Akron Archives.)

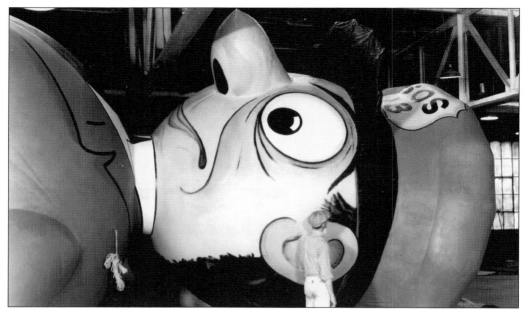

Police on duty numbered 3,600 on the cloudless Thanksgiving Day of November 25, 1937, as the 14th parade began its journey to Macy's. The mayor of New York City, Fiorello LaGuardia, and his wife and two children became part of the spectacle-watching crowd at 34th Street. Portrayed by a 63-foot-tall balloon, Officer SOS 13 made his first parade appearance. (Courtesy of Bill Smith collection.)

The Nantucket Sea Monster gets his sea legs in the 1937 parade. (Courtesy of *New York Daily News*.)

Officer SOS 13, one of New York City's and Macy's finest, was cheered every step of the way in 1937. The 35 handlers that controlled the officer's forward movement had a difficult time with the returning sea serpent. This water–loving monster needed 8,300 cubic feet of helium to help him stay aloft and out of his element. Men with handlebar mustaches, which the press called "the most imposing since Diamond Jim Brady's day," escorted the Man on the Flying Trapeze. Also appearing was Pinocchio, one of the most oddly designed balloons to join the ranks of the parade. (Courtesy of *New York Daily News*.)

The balloons, which had arrived from Goodyear in Akron, Ohio, were inflated under tents on 110th Street early on November 24, 1938, and the parade was ready to go. After assembling at the Cathedral of St. John the Divine, the parade kicked off from Central Park West and 106th Street at 1:00 p.m. and proceeded smartly along for nearly two hours. (Courtesy of Macy's.)

The estimated one million people lining the streets and leaning out of apartment windows delighted in two new giant balloons in 1938. They were nothing short of masterpieces. The first was a helium and rubber re-creation of Walt Disney's Ferdinand the Bull, who carried a bunch of flowers in his left hoof since the cartoon Ferdinand loved sitting in a field just smelling the flowers. The other new balloon was the Big Man, Little Man balloon. (Courtesy of Goodyear Tire and Rubber Company collection, University of Akron Archives.)

After Ferdinand the Bull passed 34th Street in 1938, Santa Claus mounted the marquee, delivered a Christmas greeting, and signaled for the store windows draped in red and green canvas to be unveiled. The crowd then rushed to see the displays of mechanical toys behind the glass. (Courtesy of Bill Smith collection.)

The Big Man, Little Man balloon, designed by a 12-year-old boy from Brooklyn, joined parade veterans Pinocchio and the huge Christmas stocking in 1938. The balloons had two hurdles to clear: elevated train tracks at Columbus Avenue and at 53rd Street. One by one they were thrown on their backs and rallied on by the crowds. (Courtesy of *New York Daily News*.)

In 1939, a grandly patriotic Uncle Sam, standing 75 feet tall from stars-and-stripes hat to feet, held the distinction of being the tallest balloon to appear in the parade to date. His 30-odd handlers, each dressed in a costume from a different foreign nation, guided Sam along some 12 feet off the ground. Since the Sixth Avenue elevated train line at 53rd Street had been demolished, the balloons could be bigger, as they no longer had to be maneuvered underneath the overhead tracks. But Uncle Sam was still in for trouble. The *Herald Tribune* reported "Uncle Sam springs a deficit" after the balloon's precious supply of helium slowly started to escape about 11:45 a.m. Causing only a short pause in the parade, Sam acquired more helium and quickly regained his stature. Bringing up the rear, the huge, jolly Santa balloon moved gracefully along the route. Although Uncle Sam stood head and shoulders above Santa, it was duly reported that Santa was the biggest balloon, as measured by helium volume. (Courtesy of *New York Daily News.*)

The Scarecrow was there in 1939, providing support for his Oz compatriot the Tin Man, appearing without his ax, who was taking time off from saving Dorothy from the Wicked Witch of the West. Ole King Cole, the merry Macy's soul, made his royal appearance this year as a float. (Courtesy of *New York Daily News*.)

With the 17th annual parade getting ready to step off, newspapers on Wednesday, November 20, 1940, heralded the first appearance by the Man of Steel: Superman. This was to be the first of a trio of Superman balloons that Macy's enlisted to protect the citizens along the parade route. With him in the air, criminals were nowhere to be found. His crude cartoon appearance was a far cry from today's superhero. Central Park West was reportedly lined six deep in anticipation of the parade. The crowd estimates were placed at one million. All were eager to watch Superman's flight to Macy's. They were astonished by his 23-foot chest and 8-foot smile. A total of 50 handlers, costumed in green and yellow, guided Superman down the route. The parade also featured an alphabet theme that year. Examples included *A* for America, *B* for Babar the Elephant, *G* for the genie sprawled along a great float with Arabians in attendance, and *K* for Captain Kidd with a swashbuckling crew of pirates crossing swords. The sun went behind the clouds for a while but came out again by noon, reflecting off the brightly colored floats. One such float, Neptune and the Mermaids, was a real crowd pleaser. (Courtesy of Bill Smith collection.)

50

Laffo, a 75-foot clown transformed from the previous year's Tin Man, joined the parade in 1940 wearing a yellow-and-green clown suit. Other balloons included parade veteran Uncle Sam and a 35-foot-long, green-and-pink polka-dotted hippopotamus. The 2,000 police officers at the parade reportedly wore grins as large as those beaming from the crowds. (Courtesy of Bill Smith collection.)

Here is an eye-catching advertisement from 1941. (Courtesy of Macy's.)

The 1941 parade was supposed to feature seven giant balloons. Before the parade got under way, however, the 50-foot-tall Santa Claus balloon collapsed, causing disappointment among the estimated 50,000 spectators at the 106th Street starting point. As the Santa balloon was taken out of the procession, 17 floats, 7 drum and bugle corps, and the remaining 6 balloons began the annual voyage down to Macy's. (Courtesy of *New York Daily News.*)

A huge sea serpent and a giant hippopotamus made the trek without any problems in 1941. Some of the non–balloon parade favorites included Jiminy Cricket and Monstro the Whale, clowns, and jugglers. (Courtesy of Bill Smith collection.)

*Three*

# THE 1940S
## THE BIG BALLOONS ENLIST

With every newspaper page bringing forth details on the war in Europe, the country was in an unsettled state. Outrage over each act of aggression perpetrated by the Nazis was building, yet the American people were assured by the politicians that the United States would not enter the war.

The weather on November 20, 1941, was described as summerlike, and the general consensus was that it was one of the best parade days in the 18-year history of the event. Despite the warm weather, many in the crowd were decked out in furs and topcoats. The one million spectators—the crowds were said to be 10 to 12 people deep in some locations—witnessed fantasy become reality, with the highflying Dumbo balloon leading the pack. Superman, the star of the previous parade, had gone through surgery at Goodyear and returned this year as a football player. Disney's Reluctant Dragon was not the least bit reluctant to greet those waving to him, and all went swimmingly for the 52-foot-long Goldfish.

Once Santa Claus arrived at Macy's and took his place on a throne atop the marquee, the ceremonies began, welcoming him to New York City. Dinah Shore sang at the marquee at 34th Street, setting the tone with Christmas carols. After the band played "The Star-Spangled Banner," Santa climbed into a window on his way to a party for the children of Macy's executives and guests.

After passing the review stands, the parade headed toward Seventh and Eighth Avenues, and the task of breaking down the floats began. The balloons were deflated and sent back to Macy's warehouse in Long Island City for a yearlong nap. Santa Claus appeared in a second-story window of the store to wish the crowd a merry Christmas.

Just after Thanksgiving, on December 7, 1941, the unthinkable happened: Pearl Harbor was bombed. The country, in shock from the Sunday-morning attack, listened on December 8, 1941, as Pres. Franklin D. Roosevelt announced in his historic speech that the United States would enter the war. America was thrust into World War II. Countless men, young and not so young, joined the armed forces. Women served in the Red Cross and took factory jobs to help keep tanks and airplanes rolling off the assembly lines. Stars of the stage and screen performed for the troops. The nation came together in a way not seen before or since.

For four years, the country sacrificed. While U.S. soldiers fought overseas, the nation bought war bonds, rationed food and gasoline, and collected scrap metal. All metal of value was made into airplanes, tanks, and other vehicles. Another important material, needed for the manufacture of tires and life rafts, was rubber. On November 13, 1942, Macy's Jack Straus donated the giant balloons to Mayor Fiorello LaGuardia. The dragon balloon was inflated with air, since helium was also an important commodity during the war, and in dramatic fashion, the mayor plunged a knife into the dragon. Thus, Macy's balloon stars became 650 pounds of valuable rubber.

The year 1945 marked the end of the war and the return of the soldiers, as well as the return of the Macy's Thanksgiving Day Parade. The GI Bill helped soldiers' families settle into new homes, and, for many, the American Dream became reality. The suburbs were the destination for relocation. Prosperity abounded. Television promised movie-quality images (on six-inch screens) as the country tuned in to watch *The Milton Berle Show, Howdy Doody,* or just test patterns. After a three-year postponement, the Macy's Thanksgiving Day Parade was back. (This was the first parade since 1926 that was not designed by Tony Sarg, who had passed away in 1942. He was sorely missed.) Headlines the day after described the parade's return: "Macy Parade Brings Fairyland Back From War-Time Dug-out," proclaimed the *New York Herald Tribune,* and the *New York Daily News* called the parade "Peace-Time Thanksgiving—With All the Trimmings." The press estimated that nearly two million people lined the route to view the first postwar parade. Macy's estimated that since the last parade in 1941, one million children had been born, resulting in many first-time viewers who witnessed Macy's magic with wide-eyed wonderment.

The parade's 20th edition in 1946 stepped off at 10:00 a.m. Near-freezing temperatures greeted 1947's parade, but they were made bearable by the glorious mid-autumn sunshine, which helped to swell the crowd. Many spectators hung out of windows or stood upon theater marquees and rooftops to get a better view. Six bands marched that year, including the 72-piece Rockville Centre High School band and the returning Ferko String Band. The honor of leading the procession went to the Hoboken American Legion Post No. 107. Walking down Central Park West, the Legionnaires were cheered on by the crowd every step of the way. With *Miracle on 34th Street* enjoying a solid release, Macy's presented the crowd with another holiday gift in the persons of Maureen O'Hara and John Payne, who greeted the crowd at Macy's Herald Square marquee.

For the November 25, 1948, parade, nine bands provided music, and Howdy Doody introduced Santa Claus at Macy's. A crowd nearing 2.35 million—then the largest to date—lined the route. Along with the bands, 16 floats and 6 huge balloons held places in the parade. The day featured bright sunshine and a perfect blend of fairy-tale and funny-paper characters.

The 1,600 policemen on duty tended to look the other way when youngsters ducked under the barricades to get a better view of the eye-popping and fantastic sights passing in front of them. Santa's float, making its way into Herald Square, consisted of a regal throne with six soldiers providing escort. Atop the marquee, Santa shouted "Merry Christmas," and then, with a pull of a string, the Christmas windows were unveiled, presenting the story of the Little Lost Chord.

One of the biggest fans of the parade that year was William O'Dwyer, the mayor of New York City. Sitting in the grandstands at 34th Street, O'Dwyer was overheard saying, "It's a wonderful parade!" When asked for a statement, he replied, "Make a Thanksgiving statement? Why, just take a look at the faces of those kids . . . that's my statement."

The 23rd parade in 1949 was the biggest to date, featuring 5 of the famous huge balloons, 16 floats, 10 championship bands, and clowns, clowns, and more clowns. The day was bright and sunny, with a chill in the air. At 10:00 a.m., a majorette from the Rockville Centre High School Band raised her baton and the band began to play, signaling the start of the parade.

In 1950, the 24th edition featured 15 magnificent floats, 11 championship marching bands with 700 musicians, and 25 comedy acts. The weather was chilly, with bursts of snow flurries providing a holiday air. An estimated 1.5 million people jammed the streets, peered out of windows, stood on rooftops, and huddled under blankets, cheering each sight passing before them. The parade featured a large number of celebrities, including Bobby Benson and his Cowboy Troupe, Bert Parks, who later became famous for hosting the Miss America Pageant, and Jimmy Durante, who had the honor of being grand marshal. Durante, a national treasure even then, was dressed to the nines in a red topper, yellow trousers, and a blue Chesterfield coat. As he traveled the route, he threw out the types of lines he was famous for: "Hurry up I'm ready for another photograph. Dem drums is drivin' me crazy. Whudaya want? The weather is all right here but at the end of my nose it's snowin." He and his remarks received the most press the next day.

The parade arrived in Herald Square at 11:15 a.m. Macy's sponsored a contest to name the new fish balloon that year. The winner received a 1951 Ford and a television set. Santa arrived at Macy's, where he joined Parks, Durante, Hopalong Cassidy, and Boris Karloff in holiday greetings to the crowd. After proclaiming "A happy Thanksgiving to you all and a merry Christmas," Santa told the children not to eat too much that day so that they would not be too full to enjoy the holiday.

# "WE'VE ENLISTED!"

# THERE WILL BE

# NO PARADE

# THIS THANKSGIVING

WE Macy balloons have always stood for peace and plenty of fun for all. We were a waving and bobbing symbol of democracy at play. We figured in a parade devoted to laughter and shenanigans. Four never marched in our ranks. There wasn't a grownup or a gun in the whole shebang. The 2,000,000 people who came to enjoy the show were peace lovers too. But now we're a war to win, and we've enlisted, to help make the world safe for future parades full of merriment and good will.

We are turning ourselves over, body and soul, with no strings attached, to the New York City Salvage Committee. Destined for the rubber scrap pile, we will perhaps find our way into tires for tanks, or maybe life rafts. Wherever we're most needed, we'll be glad to serve our country—though we can't help wishing we could float over Hirohito's palatial shack, and frighten him out of his kimono. We'd like to act as barrage balloons, too, and hang around New York or London. But it's up to the armed forces. What they say goes. And whatever assign-

ment we draw, we'll swell with pride (helium or no helium) knowing that we're going to help defeat Hitler and his classes.

Our public, though disappointed that the parade will not parade, will be glad that Macy's has donated us to the war effort. The helium that used to inflate us will be saved, also the metal cylinders in which it came. The tires and gas, too, that conveyed the enormous trucks and floats down Broadway, will be spared for more important jobs. And we know you'll agree it is wise not to attract a crowd of 2,000,000 people in times when New York's Finest are needed to guard warehouses and docks.

So we're wishing you a fine dinner, and as we go to join up, we'll be looking forward to that glorious Thanksgiving Day when our descendants will parade down Central Park West and Broadway, while millions cheer. Boy! Will that be a Thanksgiving!

P.S. Our famous mechanical windows, designed by Russell Patterson, will perform as usual, starting on Thanksgiving Day at 9 A.M. This year the show's called "THE FUNNY PAGE PARADE," and you'll recognize lots of your closest friends in the 26 Scenes!

# MACY*S

With the nation at war in 1942, it was a sad time for America. There was no parade that year. (Courtesy of Macy's.)

With the country still at war, 1943 also passed without a parade. (Courtesy of Macy's.)

The third year without a parade came in 1944, but there was considerable hope for the next year. (Courtesy of Macy's.)

After a rainy and gloomy morning in November 1945, the weather broke, providing a perfect day for parade watching. From the first glimpse of the giant balloons bobbing down the streets of the city, it seemed as if there had never been a time without the parade. Once the parade stepped off, it was two and a half hours of delight. Six mounted policemen led the march, followed by a delegation of children, the sons and daughters of the William E. Sheridan Post of the American Legion. The army band led the procession, followed by six bands spaced out along the line of march. Floats included a flag float that paid tribute to the Allies, Humpty Dumpty sitting atop his brick wall, and a cornstalk-decorated scarecrow mounted on a spring. Adding to the autumnal atmosphere was a 40-foot-long pumpkin float, decorated with fence posts and leaves, that featured a square-dance caller and a hillbilly band. (Courtesy of Macy's.)

In 1945, after the Giant Pumpkin balloon said "pumpkin pie" to all and the parade passed by, the Christmas windows were unveiled. The animated scene showed Alice in Wonderland with a series of 26 miniature floats that revolved through the display. (Courtesy of *New York Daily News.*)

The 17-foot-tall turkey held a place of honor in 1945. American Indians in full feathered headdress provided thrills for the young cowboys and cowgirls in attendance. Also capturing the young ones' attention were a rocket ship, which featured a man from Mars, and a seal, which balanced a ball upon its nose. (Courtesy of *New York Daily News.*)

Bobo the Hobo Clown, who was 38 feet wide and 44 feet tall and dressed in a colorful clown coat, needed 6,000 cubic feet of helium to keep him clowning above Broadway in 1945. A 35-foot-tall triple-scoop Ice-Cream Cone was kept afloat by 3,500 cubic feet of helium. The fifth balloon in 1945 was a lovable 40-foot-tall teddy bear with a huge ribbon around its neck. In 1946 the parade's route was altered, with the starting point at 77th Street and Central Park West. (Courtesy of *New York Daily News.*)

This clown was a crowd pleaser in 1945, but the place of honor still belonged to Santa Claus as he made his way to Herald Square on a float that carried his sleigh, which was packed for the big trip to every child's home on Christmas Eve. Awaiting his arrival in Herald Square, an honor guard of red-coated soldiers stood at attention. (Courtesy of *New York Daily News*.)

Appropriately, the pilgrim passes in front of the Mayflower Hotel during the 1946 parade. (Courtesy of *New York Daily News*.)

Getting plenty of publicity in 1946 was Bill "Hopalong Cassidy" Boyd. Popular in the movies, he soon enjoyed renewed popularity due to television. Making his first parade appearance, he traversed the route atop his faithful Arabian steed, Topper; his silver-encrusted saddle was pegged at $10,000. He was followed by a group of cowboys and cowgirls and a covered wagon. After them came the tumblers, a trampoline float, the Three Men in a Tub float, the Ferko String Band, and the pirate ship navigated by Donald Duck and Pinocchio. (Courtesy of Macy's.)

After this pilgrim made his way down the parade route in 1946 and wished everyone a happy Thanksgiving, an old jalopy—a "Comedy" Ford—made its way down the streets, backfiring along every foot of pavement. The Old Lady in the Shoe also passed by with her 10 problem children. (Courtesy of Bill Smith collection.)

Beside the Panda balloon is a confectioner's delight, the 46-foot-tall candy cane. This photograph was taken in 1946. (Courtesy of Goodyear Tire and Rubber Company collection, University of Akron Archives.)

Balloon stars wait to make their parade appearance in 1946. It took 4,000 cubic feet of helium to fill the 40-foot-tall Pilgrim balloon and 3,600 cubic feet of helium to fill the 38-foot-tall Panda balloon. Next in line were the Ice-Cream Cone and the Baseball Player. (Courtesy of Bill Smith collection.)

Wowing the crowd in its second
parade appearance in 1946 is
the Ice-Cream Cone balloon.
(Courtesy of Goodyear Tire and
Rubber Company collection,
University of Akron Archives.)

The next balloon to make its way
along the parade route in 1946 was the
46-foot-tall Baseball Player, who had
formerly been Bobo the Hobo Clown.
(Courtesy of Bill Smith collection.)

Maureen O'Hara hugs Natalie Wood in a scene from a holiday classic that had a bit of Macy's magic, too. (*Miracle on 34th Street,* copyright 1947 by Twentieth Century Fox. All rights reserved.)

Photographs such as this one could have been taken any year. Only the old-fashioned street signal tells us this is 1947. (Courtesy of *New York Daily News*.)

The policeman of 1947's parade had flown in 1945 as a clown and in 1946 as the Baseball Player. In 1948, he became Harold the Fireman. The real treat that year, however, was the arrival of Santa Claus. Once Santa arrived at Macy's and took his honored position on a throne, he said, "A merry Christmas to you all and a happy New Year!" (Courtesy of Bill Smith collection.)

After the 1947 march (pictured above), there could be no denying that Macy's had once again provided the perfect present for young and old alike. The Ice-Cream Cone from 1946 became the Gnome in 1947. (Courtesy of Goodyear Tire and Rubber Company collection, University of Akron Archives.)

Yo! Ho! Ho! and the Macy's Thanksgiving Day Parade. The Pirate balloon is pictured here in 1947. (Courtesy of Goodyear Tire and Rubber Company collection, University of Akron Archives.)

Harold the Fireman is flying high in the 1948 parade. (Courtesy of Bill Smith collection.)

In 1948, the honor of kicking off the parade went to the Hoboken Post No. 107 American Legion Drum and Fife Corps. Behind them came Harold the Fireman. Harold, who required 6,700 cubic feet of helium to keep his suspenders on, made his way to Macy's despite the fact that he kept losing helium through his feet. After receiving additional helium, he resumed his fireless drill. When the fireman had cleared a path, a float featuring a whale spouting water made its way down the route, accompanied by six men carrying red umbrellas to protect themselves from getting soaked. The float was pegged as a standout by the crowd. Another float labeled "spectacular" by the press was the Mississippi River Showboat, which was a triple-decker. As the boat traveled, smoke rose from its twin smokestacks, its paddle wheel turned, and its whistle tooted. The Alice in Wonderland float also had many fans. It featured all of Alice's friends from the looking glass and carried Howdy Doody and Bob Smith. The Indian Head float came next with an escort of American Indians. (Courtesy of Goodyear Tire and Rubber Company collection, University of Akron Archives.)

This cheerful balloon is clowning down Central Park West in 1949. (Courtesy of *New York Daily News*.)

In 1948, two other balloons—a huge green-and-yellow crocodile (which had the honor of preceding Santa Claus) and a monkey hanging from a trapeze—completed the inflated contingent. The only balloon incident happened just before the start of the parade, when the monkey had one of its legs punctured. Despite the lack of helium, he managed to finish the parade. (Courtesy of Goodyear Tire and Rubber Company collection, University of Akron Archives.)

Television star Milton Berle had the honor of being the grand marshal in 1949 and attended the parade costumed as Father Knickerbocker. Berle was doing fine until he reached 47th Street. As he leaned over the throne, he took a tumble, but he quickly regained his balance and came up smiling. (Courtesy of *New York Daily News*.)

As each balloon passed by in 1949, anticipation grew for the appearance of Santa Claus, who, outfitted with a microphone hidden under his beard, proclaimed "Merry Christmas." Mayor William O'Dwyer attended, again viewing the parade from the grandstand on 34th Street. Milton Berle, who arrived at the reviewing stand in Herald Square about 20 minutes before Santa did, had the honor of addressing the audience. "On behalf of R. H Macy's, and I'd like to be half of Macy's, I wish you a happy Thanksgiving and a merry Christmas," Berle said. Santa arrived at Macy's at noon. He climbed the marquee and addressed the crowd, saying simply, "I greet you all." With that short speech he signaled to unveil the Christmas windows, revealing a display entitled "To Grandfather's House We Go" that featured 26 miniature moving parade floats portraying Christmas in the country. (Courtesy of *New York Daily News*.)

This high-kicker is stepping off the parade in 1949. (Courtesy of *New York Daily News*.)

Two of the balloons encountered difficulties in 1949. The Dachshund had problems at 47th Street, and the crocodile had his at 74th Street. Both were quickly repaired and returned to full flying speed. (Courtesy of Goodyear Tire and Rubber Company collection, University of Akron Archives.)

Hot Dog! The Dachshund welcomed Hopalong Cassidy and Topper, who made their second parade appearance in 1950. (Courtesy of *New York Daily News*.)

As trumpets sounded, Cinderella's coach came into view, carrying Cinderella, the prince, and the fairy godmother along the route of the 1950 parade. Bobby Benson and his cowboy troupe whooped it up for all the young fans in the crowd. The Toy Soldier balloon kept a watchful eye on the masses and on the other balloons that held sway in the line of march—the Gnome, the Clown, and the unnamed fish. The St. Bernadette Cadet Corps signaled the arrival of the bad man of the movies, Boris Karloff. Karloff was getting good notices as Captain Hook in the Broadway production of *Peter Pan*. He rode atop the Pirate Ship float in full Captain Hook costume, accompanied by a swashbuckling crew. After arriving at the Macy's marquee, Jimmy Durante provided colorful commentary for the crowd gathered in Herald Square. Santa Claus rode atop a float that featured a red, blue, and gold sleigh driven by eight reindeer. (Courtesy of Goodyear Tire and Rubber Company collection, University of Akron Archives.)

# Four

# THE 1950S
# TV, ROCK-AND-ROLL,
# AND GIANT SPACEMEN

As war clouds gave way to bright, optimistic skies, America emerged as a nation empowered. Presidents Harry Truman and Dwight D. Eisenhower were the leaders of the free world as millions of servicemen returned to work, got married, and fathered an unprecedented number of children. The Korean War took its toll, and Cold War temperatures rose and dipped. Still, life for many was good again. New housing was cheap. *I Love Lucy* was on the small screen, and Marilyn Monroe was on the big screen. The only troubles were fears of communism and an uproar over a hip-shaking pop star named Elvis Presley. Television quickly surpassed radio as the household's electronic center. Through increasing use of this new medium via NBC-TV, Macy's began to enlarge its stage and added more television celebrities to the parade. Since its debut in the Roaring Twenties, the parade seemed to have come full circle in this cheerful, chicken-in-every-pot decade.

Starting off a new decade of parades on November 22, 1951, was Bert Lahr, star of Broadway's *Two on the Aisle* but known for generations as the Cowardly Lion from the classic movie *The Wizard of Oz*. Perched on the golden American Eagle float and dressed as Captain Universe, Lahr stepped off from Central Park West to the blare of the Rockville Centre High School Band. Meanwhile, along the bend of Columbus Circle, crowds witnessed a fish out of water as the big fish balloon swayed its fins. Filled with 6,500 cubic feet of helium, the fish hooked itself on a lamppost and sprang a leak. By Eighth Avenue, the fish had wilted to the pavement.

Kicking off the parade on November 27, 1952, as grand marshal was Brooklyn's own famous bus driver—the Great One himself—Jackie Gleason. His CBS variety show presenting *The Honeymooners* was hitting its stride. The parade started its journey with his familiar refrain of "Away we go!" Making a return appearance was Mighty Mouse, flying high above the carnival shenanigans of Jack Sterling, ringmaster from the *Big Top TV Show,* and clowns Bozo and Lassy. Nearby was the Showboat float with southern belles and their beaus dancing about. In the wake of the Showboat followed television's Jock Mahoney astride his horse Rawhide. Other celebrity sightings were Oscar-winning actress Mercedes McCambridge of *All the King's Men,* Eddie Albert (before he starred in *Green Acres*), Toni Campbell, Dagmar from *Mama,* and master of ceremonies Garry Moore. The parade celebrated the movies by adding a float devoted to the 1953 release of the Columbia Pictures film *The 5,000 Fingers Of Dr. T.*

In 1952, parade crowds reached record levels of 2.25 million. The throngs of happy spectators grinned at the antics of vaudeville performers Aunt Matilda and Uncle Hirman, waved to the Chiquita banana in her tropical garden, and looked above to the big fish (flying successfully this year), the teddy bear, and the crocodile balloons. The parade and Santa successfully reached their destination while the Sewanhaka High School Band, one of 11 championship bands, performed a rousing rendition of "Buckle Down, Winsocki."

Sunny skies and soothing autumn winds greeted two million adults and youngsters on November 26, 1953, for the 27th parade. For the second year in a row, Macy's picked a king of television comedy as its exalted grand marshal. Stepping onto the regal American Eagle float on 77th Street was Sid Caesar of *Your Show of Shows.* Behind him was his partner in comedy, Imogene Coca, and behind her was the oblong Dachshund balloon.

The parade's theme for 1954 was "For the Joy of Children Everywhere." To make good on that promise, Macy's invited one of the most popular comedy teams, Bud Abbott and Lou Costello. They arrived at the assembly point Thanksgiving morning after wrapping up work on *Abbott and Costello Meet the Mummy* the day before. The lanky straight man and chubby clown were cast as madcap ringmasters on the parade's elaborate Circus float. With its calliope bellowing out carnival music, the roving three-ring tent on wheels was flanked by three elephants. While Abbott and Costello provided star power, the parade found room for a return appearance by Sid Caesar as Captain Noah. Another actor portraying a folklore figure was former child star Jackie Cooper as Jim Hawkins on the Long John Silver float. Movie star Virginia Mayo was the Queen of Hearts. Dressed in red satin and black velvet trimmed with ermine, the actress reportedly braved the weather with unglamorous long johns. Another actress was Oscar-winner Judy Holiday of *Born Yesterday*, who waved to the crowds from her winter holiday float.

Not every float bore a celebrity. The Peter Pan float hosted a young girl of Greek parentage from Albania. The girl and her family were among other refugees brought into the country by Macy's with consent by the U.S. State Department. Throughout the decade, parade floats were increasingly drawing rave reviews, thanks to the new art designer, William Tracy, a former member of Ringling Brothers and Barnum & Bailey Circus. The 34th Street Christmas windows that awaited Santa Claus that year were a charming sight featuring the Littlest Snowman. Santa's simple wave brought smiles to the crowds.

The parade turned 30 on November 22, 1956. Gusty winds whipped the Midtown streets and wreaked havoc on the balloons. The grand marshal was cowboy Roy Rogers, who corralled the movies and television. He and his wife and favorite leading lady, Dale Evans, along with their children, rode a chuck wagon flanked by a sheriff's posse astride 15 golden horses. Another Saturday matinee idol in the line of march was Flash Gordon himself, Buster Crabbe, who, accompanied by his son Cullen, appeared costumed as his television character Captain Gallant of the Foreign Legion.

Much of the parade's visual spectacle was provided by the floats. One gorgeous addition was a three-part circus tableau that featured a crescent-shaped bandwagon pulled by an oversized toy giraffe whose mane was comprised of 50,000 amber straws. Parade watchers caught a glimpse of Basil Rathbone, the screen's immortal Sherlock Holmes, on the Starlight Starbright float. Parading by for comic strip fans were the cast from the Broadway musical *Li'l Abner,* headlining Edie Adams and Stubby Kaye (Marryin' Sam). Next was Spike Jones.

By the late 1950s, the Western had evolved into television's most popular genre, so Macy's chose Hugh O'Brian, star of *Wyatt Earp,* as the 1957 grand marshal. Under calm skies on November 28, O'Brian led off the march, while Hopalong Cassidy rode Topper. The parade changed its route that year due to construction work. Instead of taking the usual turn onto Broadway past Columbus Circle, marchers headed east along Central Park South and down Seventh Avenue. Broadway was picked up after Times Square. Santa arrived at Macy's despite the detour.

"Westerns, Westerns, Westerns!" was the theme on November 27, 1958, as the parade opened with a trio of gun-toting, horse-riding television cowboys. The first man, in his ten-gallon hat, was Dale Robertson, star of NBC's *Tales of Wells Fargo.* He was followed by Robert Horton of NBC's *Wagon Train.* Nearby on his saddle was George Montgomery, the hero of *Cimarron City,* also shown on NBC. The trio reportedly drew hoots and hollers from fans.

The skies were clear, but a 28-mile-per-hour wind picked a fight with the parade's returning balloon favorite, Popeye. In a pre-parade battle that rivaled his fisticuffs with Bluto, the sailor punctured his arm. That left only the Giant Spaceman and the Toy Soldier balloons to save the day. With this, the 32nd parade returned to the previous route down Broadway.

Greeting parade day in 1959 were strong winds, which again whipped the ropes of the giant balloons, their massive frames swaying from curb to curb. Gorgeous Gobbler, the Spaceman, and

Popeye all survived. At the start of the line of march was legendary former child star Shirley Temple. By then 31 years old, the future U.S. ambassador braved the cold in white mink; she was accompanied by her three children on the elaborate Storybook float. Cowboys, of course, were also featured attractions. Riding in on his horse, fresh from the set of ABC-TV's *The Rifleman* series, was Chuck Conners.

Other celebrities braving the cold on floats included comedienne Pat Carroll, who portrayed Mother Goose, and musical princess Connie Francis as Cinderella. Suiting up as Old King Cole was musical comedy star Jules Munshin, and sailing the *Good Ship Emily Morgan* (the name of Macy's founder Roland H. Macy's whaling boat) was comedian Bobby Clark as Captain Macy. Next to Clark was nine-year-old Emily Severance Grinnell, the great-great-granddaughter of Emily Morgan.

As the marchers approached Times Square, the sounds of drums and slide trombones from high school bands filled the air. Providing a touch of class that year was the New York City Center Light Opera Company, singing in harmony on the colorful Carousel float. Supplying legs and taps were the Rockettes, whose spotlight in Herald Square became a tradition. The freezing-cold marchers finished the day by bringing Santa to Herald Square.

Cowboys led the line of march for the November 24, 1960, parade with the cast of the year's most popular NBC-TV show, *Bonanza*. It was one of the earliest shows shot in color, and the series helped RCA, then NBC's owner, sell millions of color television sets. Trotting out on their saddles were the Cartwrights of the Ponderosa: Lorne Greene, Pernell Roberts, Dan Blocker, and Michael Landon. Adding music to the triumphant ride was the High School Mountain Lion Band of Charleston, West Virginia. Stepping onto the Mexican Fiesta float and promoting the upcoming movie *Pepe* was the versatile Shirley Jones, the future star of *The Partridge Family*. Riding the Royal float was young Lori Martin, star of NBC-TV's *National Velvet*, based on the 1944 film classic.

Before Santa's arrival, Macy's provided a tasteful layer of icing with the Christmas Tree float, which featured the Radio City Music Hall Corps de Ballet. An important addition to the behind-the-scenes crew working on the parade took place this year. Manfred G. Bass, fresh out of military service, joined the staff of William Tracy's company, which was responsible for producing the floats for the parade at the time. While Bass's background was in sculpture, he was also a master artist, master carpenter, and master welder. He was a man with an imagination who was ready to break the mold of float building and bring the parade to a new glorious and artistic level by transforming fantasy into reality. During a decade in which conventionality was the ideal, the Macy's Thanksgiving Day Parade had quietly evolved from a hometown block party into a professionally produced network variety show. The parade, more than ever, became a pop culture event in which the stars came out to shine.

The advertisement from 1951 announced fun for everyone. (Courtesy of Macy's.)

At the 1951 parade, it felt like the circus was in town: carnival barkers beckoned as jugglers and acrobats performed around the gold-and-silver Ferris wheel. Flying to the jaunty sounds of circus music was the decade's first superstar balloon, the fabulous Mighty Mouse. (Courtesy of *New York Daily News*.)

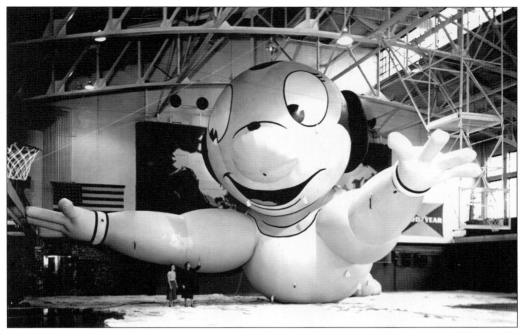

With his arms outstretched 42 feet, his eyes as wide as sunshine, and a smile one could fall into, the 70-foot Mighty Mouse balloon closely resembled his cartoon counterpart and made a charming, majestic presence. He is seen here in 1951. (Courtesy of Goodyear Tire and Rubber Company collection, University of Akron Archives.)

Hovering above the syncopated steps of the young marchers in 1951 was the massive Toy Soldier, followed by winter's famous Frosty the Snowman. Behind the happy snowman were his trusty little attendants in glittery white and royal red. Little Bo Peep and Mistress Mary were close on his heels. (Courtesy of Bill Smith collection.)

Soon a massive shadow fell over the city streets, and the skies darkened as the parade entered the atomic age in 1952. The Spaceman, seen here in Akron, debuted high above with his slow horizontal lurch. This man of the future wore a helmet, space boots, and oxygen tanks. The spectacular creation was filled with 38,000 cubic feet of helium. (Courtesy of Bill Smith collection.)

Spectators greeting this fish out of water in Herald Square in 1953 also caught glimpses of comedienne Martha Raye astride the pirate galleon as Captain Hook. Faye Emerson, Steve Allen, Howdy Doody's Buffalo Bob Smith, and Clarabell the Clown followed. Mighty Mouse made a safe landing as the last balloon before Santa's motorized reindeer brought the jolly one to deliver his annual "Merry Christmas to you all." (Courtesy of Bill Smith collection.)

Few mishaps occurred in 1953. The Toy Soldier blew out overnight and gave up his place in the parade to the Alligator. Little Bo Peep, portrayed by actress Celeste Holm, missed her float and rejoined her sheep by way of a motorcycle and side car. Perennial favorite Hopalong Cassidy rode his horse, Topper, around the parade's clowns, bands, and Model T Fords, waving his black hat in the air. Also in the line of marchers was Wally Cox on the locomotive Casey Jones float. Most youngsters watching the parade that day probably wished to trade places with one celebrity in particular. Riding the Rocket Ship float like a pint-sized Buck Rogers was child actor Brandon De Wilde, star of the film *Shane*. Hovering for his return urban orbit was the massive Spaceman. (Courtesy of Bill Smith collection.)

Headed by the huge turkey Gorgeous Gobbler and the giant Spaceman, the balloons in 1954 were comprised of favorites from the last couple of years. The crowd of two million also greeted other attractions, such as Lassie, Howdy Doody and his gang, and the *Today Show*'s chimpanzee newscaster, J. Fred Muggs. (Courtesy of Bill Smith collection.)

Besides the friendly fish, seen here in 1955, returning balloons included the superstar Mighty Mouse and the Dachshund. The only casualty that year was the giant Spaceman, whose right arm was punctured by a lamppost on 62nd Street. Quick repairs were performed at the space dock, known to earthlings as Times Square. (Courtesy of Bill Smith collection.)

For the 1955 edition, Macy's summoned someone from the reigning comedy court—not a king but a court jester: Danny Kaye. The world-renowned star, who was promoting the film *The Court Jester,* appeared in costume atop a festive valentine float with his daughter Dena, who was dubbed queen of the parade. Marching behind Kaye were familiar sights such as Howdy Doody, Pinky Lee, and the canine Rin Tin Tin. Also traveling along Broadway were Humpty Dumpty, a Tootsie Roll float topped with a candle and flame, a rocket ship piloted by 1950s cartoon character Gerald McBoing-Boing, and a 45-foot flower garden with 500 chrysanthemum plants and a water fountain. Children were delighted by the Circus float carrying the Bouncing Bodos, an acrobatic troupe. Farther along was the Littlest Snowman float, which featured ice-skaters George Joseph and Sara Jo Bolt gliding in circles on a 7- by 20-foot rink. (Courtesy of Macy's.)

Hopalong Cassidy greets a young cowpoke before the 1955 parade. Bill Boyd, known to millions as "Hoppy," made numerous parade appearances and was a hit with the young ones and their parents, too. (Courtesy of J. Rosenthal collection.)

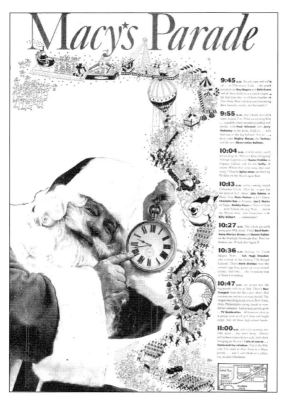

When the clock struck noon on parade day in 1956, Santa Claus arrived on a 40-foot float that was teeming with elves. The jeweled sleigh, mounted on oak-and-iron runners, had made a successful journey despite the winds. (Courtesy of Macy's.)

Mighty Mouse battles the winds at the 1956 parade. The first victim of the weather that day was the Giant Turkey balloon, which collided with a tree. The new Observer balloon, a replica of a Civil War observation balloon, saw the turkey lose its 10,000 cubic feet of helium and plunge to earth. (Courtesy of *New York Daily News*.)

Nearby, putting a smile on kids' faces, were ventriloquist Paul Winchell and his "punny" dummy Jerry Mahoney. Though they did not take a ride in this comedic backfiring car, they were in the 1956 parade. (Courtesy of *New York Daily News*.)

The five-person-deep row of spectators in 1957 gazed at skaters and at colorful floats featuring Cinderella and Sinbad the Sailor. The Cinderella float was enlivened by a romantic image of Cinderella and Prince Charming, portrayed by actors Sandra Baird and Farley Granger, dancing to a Viennese waltz. (Courtesy of *New York Daily News*.)

In 1957, the returning Circus float featured a man doing tricks atop a 28-foot pole. Other delights included the circus clown (pictured), vaudeville legend Eddy Foy Jr. on the river steamer *Amazon Queen,* and 1940s child actress Margaret O'Brien as an Arabian Nights storyteller. (Courtesy of *New York Daily News.*)

Elbowing his way through with his pumped forearms and upturned pipe was the brand-new Popeye balloon. As they had with Mighty Mouse, Goodyear employees produced a design that stuck wonderfully close to the pen-and-ink version and became a parade favorite well into the next decade. Seen here in 1957 are Goodyear's Bill Ludwick (standing) and Woody Woodward. Woodward later designed 1977's Kermit the Frog balloon. (Courtesy of Bill Smith collection.)

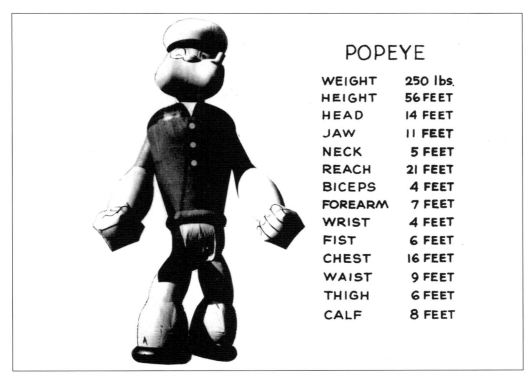

## POPEYE

| | |
|---|---|
| WEIGHT | 250 lbs. |
| HEIGHT | 56 FEET |
| HEAD | 14 FEET |
| JAW | 11 FEET |
| NECK | 5 FEET |
| REACH | 21 FEET |
| BICEPS | 4 FEET |
| FOREARM | 7 FEET |
| WRIST | 4 FEET |
| FIST | 6 FEET |
| CHEST | 16 FEET |
| WAIST | 9 FEET |
| THIGH | 6 FEET |
| CALF | 8 FEET |

Mom always said eating spinach was good for you. Just look at Popeye: he is 56 feet tall. This image is from 1957. (Courtesy of Bill Smith collection.)

Popeye flies head and shoulders above the ground at his test flight in 1957. (Courtesy of Bill Smith collection.)

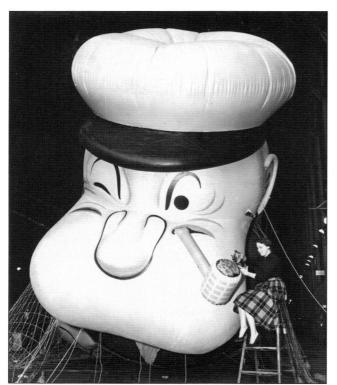

The vision for a Macy's Popeye balloon becomes reality in 1957. (Courtesy of Goodyear Tire and Rubber Company collection, University of Akron Archives.)

The test flight goes smoothly in 1957. (Courtesy of New York Daily News.)

Along the route in 1957, many city youngsters developed some sophisticated ways of getting a good view. According to a newspaper reporter, some brought boards from home, removed trash can lids, and placed the boards on top of the cans, thereby creating their own reviewing stands. The child shown here, however, took a more traditional approach, perching on her dad's shoulders. (Courtesy of *New York Daily News*.)

Along with returning favorites that included the Toy Soldier, the Gorgeous Gobbler, and the giant Spaceman, the Observer balloon made a successful run in 1957. It did, however, have a near run-in with a lamppost and a television camera truck. (Courtesy of *New York Daily News*.)

89

Rock-and-roll made some headway with the appearance of *American Bandstand* host Dick Clark, who escorted Macy's Cinderella in the 1958 parade. For older spectators who still preferred Big Band sounds, the legendary "King of Swing," Benny Goodman, made another parade appearance on the Swing float. Goodman promoted his new album, *Benny at Brussels*. Of course, there were the fabulous Rockettes (pictured above). (Courtesy of *New York Daily News*.)

Autumn's chill swept over the crowd in 1958, and parade watchers snuggled together and moved in close to see bona fide Hollywood royalty. On the Queen of the Flower float was Oscar-winner Ginger Rogers, Fred Astaire's former dance partner. (Courtesy of *New York Daily News*.)

In 1958, for the first time in the parade's history, a shortage of helium due to a federal ban narrowed the balloon roster. The Toy Soldier (pictured) and the Giant Spaceman made their trip filled with good old-fashioned air and carried by derricks. The cranes reportedly could not handle the Gorgeous Gobbler. He was put on ice to serve another year. (Courtesy of *New York Daily News*.)

In 1958, these bundled-up spectators saw Russ Tamblyn promoting MGM's movie *Tom Thumb* on the Tom Thumb float, starlet Dolores Hart on the Mother Goose float, veteran Hollywood actor Charles Ruggles as the king on the Old King Cole float, and child star Richard Eyer promoting the special-effects extravaganza *The Seventh Voyage of Sinbad* on the Sinbad the Sailor float. Besides celebrating Thanksgiving, the parade also celebrated Macy's 100th Christmas this year. (Courtesy of *New York Daily News*.)

Among the celebrities who greeted the 1.3 million spectators in 1960 was veteran comic Joe E. Brown (pictured above), who took his place alongside the New York City Center Light Opera Company on the Showboat float. (Courtesy of *New York Daily News*.)

This dragon is taking a test flight in 1960. The new balloon on the block, it was billed as "the world's happiest dragon." Flying in at 72 feet long and 20 feet high, the friendly monster nearly scared some of the toddlers nestled in their parents' arms. Yet the dragon quickly made his way into the hearts of many and became a parade favorite for years. (Courtesy of *New York Daily News*.)

Heads up! The world's happiest dragon will be flying in the 1960 parade. (Courtesy of *New York Daily News*.)

This dragon certainly is not dragging his feet in the 1960 parade. (Courtesy of *New York Daily News*.)

Bullwinkle, one of the most beloved balloons in the parade's history, was anxiously awaiting his debut in 1961. (Courtesy of Goodyear Tire and Rubber Company collection, University of Akron Archives.)

# Five

# THE 1960S

## TRAGEDIES, CHANGES, AND APOLLO SNOOPY

The decade began so innocently. Dwight D. Eisenhower, who had presided over the nation like a kindly grandfather, handed the presidency over to a dashing young man named John F. Kennedy. The musical *Camelot* sprang to mind as Kennedy and his first lady, Jacqueline, resided in the White House like royalty. "Ask not what your country can do for you. Ask what you can do for your country," was the president's rallying cry. A can-do spirit swept the nation as college students enlisted in the Peace Corps and astronauts Alan Shepard and John Glenn took the American flag into space. Meanwhile, as Elvis Presley came home from the army, millions of teenage girls swooned over pop idols such as Fabian and Frankie Avalon.

All was not rosy, however. Confronting violence and discrimination with peaceful marches, civil rights movement leaders, inspired by Dr. Martin Luther King Jr., taught generations of Americans the meaning of freedom. By 1963, difficult times were upon the country. The nation mourned the loss of President Kennedy, Lyndon Johnson assumed the presidency, and a bloody war raged in Vietnam. In pop culture, Fabian was out, the Beatles were in, and hairstyles went every which way. Welcome to the 1960s, when the Macy's Thanksgiving Day Parade became more than a holiday ritual. It was eggnog, heavy on the rum.

The cast of *Bonanza* again led the parade march on November 23, 1961. Recording star Connie Francis and television's Lori Martin also made return appearances. Newcomers included Annette Funicello, star of Walt Disney's *Babes in Toyland*, and movie actor Troy Donahue as Prince Charming on the Cinderella float. NBC's Joe E. Ross and Fred Gwynne, the bumbling officers in *Car 54, Where Are You?*, pushed their disabled police car to Herald Square with the help of a clown squad. The sports world was represented by baseball's Casey Stengel, the new manager of the New York Mets. On the Showboat float, the music world was represented by the jazz sounds of Lionel Hampton.

Although the Gorgeous Gobbler balloon lost his nose before the parade's start, the rest of day sailed along without a hitch. Sun pierced through cloudy skies as Santa arrived on his snow-covered float, which was adorned with a Christmas tree. A glowing newspaper article about parade organizer Edward Armitage Hill put smiles on the faces of the Macy's family that weekend. Hill, a Harvard-educated Bostonian who had worked on Wall Street before entering retail, now commanded a parade staff of 650 store employees. With 2,500 parade workers, the Macy's executive saw his Thanksgiving duties expand to a year-round assignment. According to press reports, Hill was to begin work on the parade "the day after Thanksgiving when he and a small committee review the day's results and discuss improvements." By summer, "all kinds of people" worked under "the fellow who has the title of director."

Macy's was pleased with the parade design crew's work. When William Tracy left the float-building business, Macy's took another step toward improving the parade by assuming the task of parade design and float construction. On November 22, 1962, despite rain and one of smallest crowds in the parade's history, the newly designed, 60-foot-tall Donald Duck balloon quacked through the wet streets. A favorite story among parade staff is the "christening" account told by parade designer Manfred Bass. In the rain of 1962, Donald Duck collected some 50 gallons of water in his hat, and "as he began to look down at you and tilt over . . . you knew you were in for another bath."

Celebrities under umbrellas that year included Jay North, the young star of *Dennis the Menace*, who buckled up on the Rocket Ship float; Disney's future leading man Dean Jones, who promoted his turn on the short-lived television show *Ensign O'Toole*; parade veteran Jimmy Durante, fresh from MGM's *Billy Rose's Jumbo*, riding a model elephant as ringmaster on the Radio City Music Hall float; Joe E. Ross and Fred Gwynne, taking another spin in Car 54; and Frank Fontaine, the *Jackie Gleason Show's* top clown, promoting his role as honorary ringmaster of the Coliseum Christmas Circus.

Sports heroes did their usual best under soggy skies. On the sports float was golf pro Arnold Palmer, Yankee Ralph Terry, football great Otto Graham, former heavyweight champion Jack Dempsey, and the "Say Hey Kid," Willie Mays. Taking the 1962 role of Prince Charming, Tony Bennett wooed the crowd on the day before his Carnegie Hall appearance. Broadway performer Carol Lawrence and Big Band drummer Gene Krupa were also on hand.

On November 22, 1963, rifle shots in Dallas, Texas, shocked America. Newly sworn-in Pres. Lyndon B. Johnson reassured the nation, but Americans grieved for John F. Kennedy. Macy's executives considered canceling the parade, but they somehow knew that a distraction from the tragedy was needed, and on November 28, a week after Kennedy's death, the parade kicked off. The mourning atmosphere lifted as people pressed against barricades and peered from apartment windows, all trying to get the best view of the parade.

Michael Landon, minus his Cartwright clan, appeared as Little Joe. Also saddling up with the posse were former New Yorker James Drury of NBC's *The Virginian* and movie villain Jack Palance, who was promoting his ABC series *The Greatest Show on Earth*. For the young set, Captain Cottle from NBC's *Ruff 'N Ready* took the helm of the Pirate Ship float.

The spotlight shined on movie star Troy Donahue, while Broadway was represented by the cast of *Here's Love*—Janis Paige, Craig Stevens, Valerie Lee, and three-time marcher Fred Gwynne. *The Wizard of Oz* star Ray Bolger also appeared. Providing laughs was comedy-album king Allan Sherman, known for his novelty hit song "Hello Mudduh, Hello Fadduh!" On the Songs of Christmas float, maestro Mitch Miller conducted his chorus. Not far away on the New York City float was his *Sing Along with Mitch* television co-star, Leslie Uggams. Drummer Gene Krupa, the Metropolitan Opera Company, and the cast of New York City Center's production of *Porgy and Bess* provided further musical attractions. The 58-degree weather helped everyone get home safely. Santa welcomed the holiday crowd, and the balloons were relieved of their helium. Macy's president David L. Yunich commented to the newspapers on his company's decision to let the show go on: "I'm glad we put it on. Just look at all the children's faces."

Winds returned for the November 26, 1964, parade. The giant balloons teetered from side to side, and the tip of a lamppost punctured Dino the Dinosaur. Popeye, the 56-foot-high sailor man, was left deflated on 77th Street. The dragon filled in for him, along with Donald Duck and Bullwinkle.

Starting the line of march was the Salute to Broadway float featuring Victor Borge, the comedian and concert pianist. The 1950s icon Fess Parker, who ignited a national mania for raccoon hats as Disney's Davy Crockett, returned in 1964 to star in NBC's *Daniel Boone*. The lanky hero stepped onto the character's log cabin float.

Other television characters in sight included CBS's new gaggle of ghouls, the Munsters. Zooming about in their hot rod, the Munster Coach, were parade returnees and former *Car 54, Where Are You?* patrolmen Fred Gwynne and Al Lewis as Herman and Grandpa. Flashing his trademark grin was funnyman Soupy Sales, and *Today Show* pioneer Dave Garroway also made an appearance. Standouts of the parade included a special Broadway float, *The Sound of Music's* puppet theater, the science-fiction float First Men in the Moon, and the Metropolitan Opera Ballet Company float. Singers Steve Lawrence and Della Reese sang, and bands played, including New Jersey's Hanover Park Golden Hornets, Florida's Mainland High School Buccaneers, and New York's Screaming Eagles Drill Team. In 1964, the telecast was advertised to be in color for the first time, and NBC paired Lorne Greene and future *Golden Girls* star Betty White as hosts.

Crowds who looked up into the skies on November 25, 1965, saw a newcomer who became a long-standing parade favorite. Spanning 63 feet with outstretched arms was canine cartoon star Underdog. The grand marshal was Macy's executive Jay Doyle, and stepping onto the NBC grandstand were Lorne Greene and Betty White. Celebrities passing before them included singer-songwriter Paul Anka, Broadway performer John Raitt (Bonnie Raitt's father), and, from the Broadway hit *The Impossible Years*, comedian Alan King. As always, the ordinary folk who marched in step also drew applause. One could not help but smile at the sight of five-year-old majorette Mary Lynne Miller, who proudly kept up with the Miller Blackhawks Herald Band of Dayton, Ohio.

The 1966 parade saw the return of America's original superhero, Superman. Also appearing was the animal-filled Noah's Ark float, which promoted 20th Century Fox's release of *The Bible*. Smokey the Bear had another successful parade in 1967. The bear's fear of raging forest fires was eased by the damp weather on November 23. The streets were soaked and the clouds were gray, but the parade's colors were still fabulous. Music was provided by stars Aretha Franklin and Dionne Warwick, and Vicki Carr was atop the Carousel float.

The cast of *You're a Good Man, Charlie Brown*, the Broadway musical hit based on Charles Schultz's groundbreaking comic strip, *Peanuts*, had a special float. The producers of the movie *Doctor Dolittle* had an elaborate contraption called the Flounder float, a re-creation of the schooner on which Doctor Dolittle sailed the high seas searching for the Great Pink Snail. Other floats included those dedicated to the upcoming 1968 World's Fair, which featured *Daniel Boone* co-star Ed Ames escorting Senorita Hemisfair, and a Lego Tivoli train with Denmark's Father Christmas and 27 small helpers. The Clydesdale horses returned, galloping alongside Santa's Candy Factory.

In the late 1960s, the creativity of the parade's staff was booming, but designers were short on space. Ray Trager of store planning encouraged Manfred Bass to find more room. Soon, the parade design crew moved into the old Tootsie Roll factory in Hoboken, New Jersey. Although the staff was limited, consisting mostly of Macy's retirees, new artists arrived to work on the parade. The young people of the Woodstock generation have often gotten a bad rap, but Manfred Bass was quick to defend those who worked on the parade: "Everybody kind of knocks 'em, but I love 'em. . . . There was some kind of magnetic energy that you would not believe—color, sculpture, everything flowed. . . .It was like breaking the mold. People were becoming less judgmental and more receiving, all of that, and it [was] reflected in the arts. We had so many different types of people, I mean every walk of life you can imagine, and they came from all over the world."

Parade spectators witnessed firsthand all of the marvelous work inspired by this new energy, and for the next decade, Manfred Bass and the parade crew broke the mold with spectacular and exciting results.

Greeting the millions of spectators during the 1968 parade was a new balloon: from pen and ink to Goodyear rubber came Snoopy. Welcoming Snoopy to the parade was the mighty Superman, a super parade presence. Lorne Greene and Betty White took the helm of the NBC broadcast, now extended to three hours. From 9:00 a.m. to 10:00 a.m., baseball's Joe Garagiola went behind the scenes for the pre-parade show.

First in the march line were Shirley Jones and Jack Cassidy, Jones's husband at the time, on the Carousel float. Standing on the Soap Box Derby float and promoting NBC's science-fiction classic *Star Trek* was William Shatner, who played Captain Kirk. Shatner's Captain Kirk became an icon as popular as Snoopy and Mickey Mouse. Also familiar to children was young Johnny Whitaker, the red-headed Jody from CBS's *Family Affair*, who road on the Snail float.

Spectators turned their heads to hear the roar of a vintage roadster with singer Jerry Vale at the wheel. Meanwhile, Bobby Vinton escorted the 1968 Junior Miss winner on the Cinderella float. From the movie *Chitty Chitty Bang Bang*, Sally Anne Howes, the film's leading lady, took a ride with the fantastical motorcar. Also in the line of march were NBC's Saturday morning characters the Banana Splits. The series featured the cry known to all youngsters of the 1960s: "Uh oh! Chongo."

Astronaut Neil Armstrong emerged from *Apollo 11* on July 20, 1969, and became the first person in history to step onto the moon's surface. The words "That's one small step for man, one giant leap for mankind" were forever etched in our minds. Celebrating this milestone in technology and achievement, Snoopy, on a sunny November 27, sported a new look. Whisking off his familiar aviation cap and goggles, the pup now wore official *Apollo* astronaut headgear, which was only fitting since, months earlier, *Apollo 10*'s lunar module had been dubbed "Snoopy."

Besides space travel, New Yorkers had something else to celebrate. The New York Mets won their first World Series championship and were now stars of the parade. Hit-makers the Four Seasons escorted the 1969 Junior Miss on Macy's new castle float, and recording artist Melanie played the Old Lady in the Shoe. Smokey the Bear had the honor of leading a battalion of volunteer firefighters from New Milford, New Jersey.

For Big Band sounds, New Year's Eve legend Guy Lombardo and his Royal Canadians got the crowd into the swing of things aboard the Broadway Belle Showboat. From the small screen was Theresa Graves of NBC's *Rowan & Martin's Laugh-In,* the irreverent show that gave us the phrase "Sock it to me!" Returning from the previous year astride the Rocking Horse float was Johnnie Whitaker from the holiday special *The Littlest Angel.* Riding with the Soap Box Derby winners was David Hartman, star of NBC's *The Bold Ones.* The littlest television tyke to appear was Marc Copage, who played Diahann Carroll's son on NBC's *Julia,* leading a series of circus floats.

Other engaging sights were the castle float, Peter Pan battling Captain Hook on the captain's ship, a dinosaur tribute to the 100th anniversary of New York's American Museum of Natural History, and the 60-foot-long Crocodile float. Disneyland was celebrated by the appearances of Snow White and the Seven Dwarfs, Mickey Mouse, Pluto, and the Three Little Pigs. Yet the most exciting moment for children was the sight of the famous Clydesdale horses pulling Santa's toy factory float.

The 1970s were ushered in with sunny skies and brisk temperatures. Hosts Lorne Greene and Betty White were now a tradition. Leading the line of march on November 26, 1970, was the Happy Dragon balloon. Return appearances were the Circus float, featuring gridiron star Rosey Grier as ringmaster; Peter Pan and the gang on Captain Hook's ship; the snaky Crocodile float; the Tortoise and the Hare; and the Broadway Belle Showboat showcasing the singing group the Lettermen.

New floats included the snowy white Ski Deck float, which provided Billy Kidd and the Hart ski team with some Macy's manufactured snow. CBS's popular *Green Acres* star Eddie Albert took his place with the international community aboard the United Nations' 25th anniversary float. The storybook greenery of the Jungle toy float (a miniature float) greeted the children along the curb, and amid the monkeys and lions was a very tropical sight: Hawaiian singer Don Ho.

Two family movies received parade exposure in 1970. Providing rhythm for the thousands along Broadway were Scatman Crothers and his Scatcats of Disney's *Aristocats. Scrooge,* the big-budget musical adaptation of Charles Dicken's classic *A Christmas Carol,* was showcased with its own holiday float. Performing his brand of country-western twang for New Yorkers was artist Hank Williams Jr.

Superman, Snoopy, and Santa all made it to Herald Square once again without a hitch. Thanks to NBC's coverage, Macy's annual event was one constant that brought joy, laughter, and holiday cheer to the whole nation.

Just right for the Mother Goose float in 1961 were Martha Wright, star of the Broadway smash *The Sound of Music,* and seven of the show's singing Von Trapp children. Also from the stage was the star of *How to Succeed in Business Without Really Trying,* Robert Morse. From the musical *Let It Ride* were Sam Levine and George Gobel. In years to come, Broadway shows became an increasingly important part of the parade's fabric. (Courtesy of *New York Daily News.*)

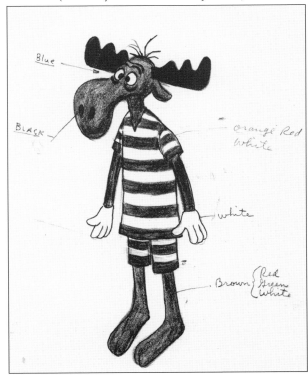

This preliminary sketch of the Bullwinkle balloon was drawn in 1961. (Courtesy of Goodyear Tire and Rubber Company collection, University of Akron Archives.)

Goodyear's Jack N. Grisak transforms a drawing into a blueprint in 1961. (Courtesy of Goodyear Tire and Rubber Company collection, University of Akron Archives.)

Here is Donald Duck in his shipping crate in 1962. Unlike the charming Donald Duck of the past who had stood up in the parades like a colorful bowling pin, the new Donald looked as if he had just stepped out of a recent Disney cartoon. (Courtesy of Goodyear Tire and Rubber Company collection, University of Akron Archives.)

Popeye's parade appearance is featured in this 1962 edition of the Goodyear News. (Courtesy of Bill Smith collection.)

Another popular cartoon icon, Bullwinkle, is pictured here in 1963. The helium-filled moose quickly become an annual parade favorite. (Courtesy of Bill Smith collection.)

In the 1963 parade, as the members of the first of 12 high school bands began twirling their batons, the line of march was led off by a float featuring the Unisphere, the modernized metal globe that became the symbol of the upcoming New York World's Fair in Flushing Meadows Park in Queens. Hovering behind, from prehistoric times, was the new Dino the Dinosaur balloon. This photograph was taken in 1963 at the fairgrounds, prior to the fair's opening in 1964. (Courtesy of Goodyear Tire and Rubber Company collection, University of Akron Archives.)

Linus the Lionhearted takes his test flight in 1964 in Akron, Ohio. At the parade, he braved the wind heroically. This royal lion was a 55-foot re-creation of the television cartoon character. He became the 84th balloon in the parade's history. Arriving at Herald Square without mishap, he was, at least in children's hearts, king of the concrete jungle. (Courtesy of Bill Smith collection.)

In 1964, Santa Claus was, as always, a star to young and old alike. (Courtesy of *New York Daily News*.)

Look, Ma, the circus is in town! This photograph is from 1965. (Courtesy of *New York Daily News*.)

Underdog is here! The helium-filled superhero, with a special *Underdog*-themed float in tow, was close in spirit to the 1950s Mighty Mouse balloon and became a signature Macy's Thanksgiving Day Parade icon for decades. Welcoming Underdog from the Goodyear Tire and Rubber Company in 1965 were Popeye, Bullwinkle, Donald Duck, Linus the Lionhearted, Dino the Dinosaur, and Elsie the Cow. (Courtesy of Lockheed Martin.)

What a pair they are: the beagle and the beetle. This photograph was taken in 1965. (Courtesy of Goodyear Tire and Rubber Company collection, University of Akron Archives.)

Underdog, seen here in 1965, is not in the doghouse but rather in the Goodyear hanger at Wingfoot Lake in Akron. (Courtesy of Goodyear Tire and Rubber Company collection, University of Akron Archives.)

Look at these swell heads! This photograph was taken in 1965. (Courtesy of Goodyear Tire and Rubber Company collection, University of Akron Archives.)

Parade workers inflate this super balloon from head to toe in 1966. (Courtesy of *New York Daily News*.)

Superman prepares for his test flight in 1966. (Courtesy of *New York Daily News*.)

Superman flew once again on November 24, 1966. It was 28 years since his debut in Action Comics, and newly fabricated, helium-filled rubber provided his muscle power. Welcoming back Superman for the parade's 40th march were fellow balloon stars Popeye, the Happy Dragon, Dino the Dinosaur, Elsie the Cow, Underdog, Bullwinkle, Linus the Lionhearted, and Donald Duck. (Courtesy of *New York Daily News*.)

A new spectacle for the 1960s audiences was the hulking frame of Smokey the Bear, seen here in 1966. The helium-filled park ranger hovered above, content with the knowledge that campfires were nowhere to be found. (Courtesy of *New York Daily News*.)

A celebrity who passed by on the Cinderella float in 1966 was singer Wayne Newton, the future "King of Las Vegas." Following behind were the majestic Clydesdale horses. Other famous people who waved to the crowds were Soupy Sales, Tony Award–winner Frankie Michaels riding aboard the Circus float, singer Teresa Brewer (pictured above), and Dusty Springfield. (Courtesy of *New York Daily News*.)

Santa arrives in New York City in 1966. (Courtesy of *New York Daily News.*)

Superman, Popeye, Bullwinkle, and Donald Duck all survived the downpour in 1967, thanks to the many Macy's workers who steered around water-logged street corners and then faced Friday-morning sniffles. Rain could not dampen the holiday spirit. (Courtesy of *New York Daily News.*)

Greeting millions in 1968 was a new balloon. Since his modest debut in *Peanuts* in 1950, Snoopy had emerged as an icon for the ages. He was greeted by smiles from everyone, old and young. Appropriately, the cast of *You're a Good Man, Charlie Brown* was back to cheer on the superstar balloon. (Courtesy of Goodyear Tire and Rubber Company collection, University of Akron Archives.)

Here is Underdog under the net and in the spotlight in 1968. Meanwhile, another cartoon icon was celebrating a milestone. Standing atop his special float that resembled a birthday cake was the 40-year-old Mickey Mouse, along with friends from the Disney studios. (Courtesy of *New York Daily News*.)

# Six

# THE 1970S
## LEISURE SUITS, DISCO, AND
## KERMIT THE FROG

Just what was the decade of the 1970s? It was a time when our nation's politicians became less revered, thanks to Watergate. It was a time when a crisscrossing social landscape seemed to transcend race and gender. A popular television commercial said it best: "You've come a long way, baby!" It was the worst of times for barbers, as hairstyles were long, shaggy, or round (the Afro). The clothes were not much better. For anyone shopping at Macy's, the choices included flopping bell-bottom pants, wide-lapel shirts splattered with every color in the rainbow, and, of course, the leisure suit, a now indescribable article of clothing. What did this era offer besides *The Godfather,* Elton John, *Jaws,* the Bee Gees, *All in the Family,* Fleetwood Mac, and *Star Wars*? Four words: Macy's Thanksgiving Day Parade.

The first parade of the new decade began on a soggy note. For days before the parade, bad weather had cursed New York. On November 25, 1971, winds and rain pelted the Manhattan streets with a vengeful fury. Conditions were so bad that Goodyear crews could not inflate the giant balloons during the night, and parade officials arrived in the early hours of Thanksgiving morning to learn that there were no balloons to fly. For children who shivered under blankets along the curbside, cold air billowing from their mouths, the loss was evident: no Happy Dragon, no Underdog, and no newly created Mickey Mouse, who had been awaiting his debut that year. This would be the first time the holiday had been without its helium friends since World War II. Nevertheless, come rain or shine, the show must go on.

Under the darkened skies, Lorne Greene and Betty White put on their best smiles for the NBC television cameras, and why not? Even with the absence of Bullwinkle, the parade boasted its usual array of spectacular floats and heart-pounding marching bands. Joining Greene and White for the parade preview show was Joe Garagiola. Added to all this "singin' in the rain" was *Tonight Show* bandleader Doc Severinsen.

Motown sensations the Temptations moved in step on the water-logged Broadway Belle Showboat. Farther down the line, the eight Clydesdale horses galloped, pulling the colorful Animal House float, which featured model lions and giraffes that captured the smiles of shivering youths. Putting on a brave face was singing-and-dancing dynamo Tommy Tune, who stood on a float promoting his new movie *The Boy Friend*. Tune later made his mark on the Broadway stage. Parade veteran Bobby Vinton sang to America's Junior Miss on the Cinderella float. Beatrix Potter's wonderful Peter Rabbit stories were re-created on a tree-lined float featuring Macy's workers dressed in costumes. Following Peter Rabbit was a mouse—Mickey Mouse, that is. Mickey appeared with Minnie, Pluto, Goofy, and Pinocchio around an amazing new float created by Macy's magicians.

Disney's Florida theme park now rivaled its famous Disneyland, and the Disney World Castle float closely resembled the Magic Kingdom's center attraction; it was a Macy's design marvel. Years later, Manfred Bass remarked, "That was really a lot of fun, working with the Disney people. They wanted us to reproduce the castle and celebrate it in the parade. We were in a sweat about the whole thing, but it was an exciting project." After being given some general information and "a little thin sketch," Bass and his crew began to develop the castle float design. It was a challenge: in addition to the creative design aspects, there were also technical needs to consider. "Our goal was to make the castle look as big and grand as possible. And yet, all parade units have to be transported from Hoboken, New Jersey, into Manhattan on the night before the parade. That means no unit can be more than twelve and a half feet high or eight feet wide in order to fit through the Lincoln Tunnel [under the Hudson River]. So how do you capture the majesty of the actual Disney World Castle given these physical restrictions? You have to create the 'magical box!'"

That magical box is similar to a giant pop-up book. Various parts of each float are designed to fold up, fold down, or telescope into position. The sides of the castle were folded out, and various elements were put in place, including the three telescoping turrets. The result was a wonderful world of Disney, courtesy of the Macy's Parade Studio team.

Bass also created a float that became a highly anticipated and welcomed sight for many years: the Turkey float that represents the parade each year in grand style. Bass is something akin to a master toymaker; in reality, he creates the world's largest puppets. The marvelous turkey, dressed in his Thanksgiving hat, collar, and tie, looks one way and nods to the people, turns his head another way and nods again, and flaps a wing on his way down to Herald Square.

Singer Lynn Anderson took her place among the zoo inhabitants (Macy's employees) on the Jungle toy float. Behind was Santa, entering his sixth decade of bringing holiday cheer to the nation. As the bearded man waded into a drenched Herald Square, Macy's president K. Wade Bennett was reportedly heard giving a sigh of relief with the words, "Well, we made it."

Temperatures were chilly on November 23, 1972, but behold—sunshine! For the thousands of youngsters along Broadway, sunshine meant the balloons would fly that year. Lorne Greene and Betty White, who had logged nearly a decade in front of the Thanksgiving Day cameras, took their place for their last parade broadcast. White was to win new fans as Sue Ann Nivens in the acclaimed *Mary Tyler Moore Show*. Helping Joe Garagiola spotlight mainstays such as the Radio City Music Hall's Rockettes was former Miss America Phyllis George.

Kicking off the march was the bright yellow Smile balloon, followed by actor John Raitt, who was making another parade appearance on the Showboat float. Next came singer Freda Payne on the Snail float and country artist Donna Fargo on the Alphabet Blocks float, a charming new parade addition featuring furry animals astride large letter blocks. Thanks to the enduring power of television, the most recognizable face seen that day was that of child actor Danny Bonaduce, the little red-headed wise guy from *The Partridge Family*, on the Doodle Bug float.

The Clydesdale horses escorted the snowman sleigh, which had a jolly snowman atop a mountain of Macy's magic snow and ice. Macy's again sailed its majestic Disney World castle float down Broadway. Another parade tradition was the sight of Peter Pan and Wendy matching wits with pirates on Captain Hook's ship float. The biggest surprise of the day came from Santa himself. Every half-block, the Santa Claus float opened its doors to reveal a Christmas tree, much to the delight of children on the sidelines.

Cold, sunny skies awaited parade watchers on November 22, 1973. NBC assembled a new team of anchors for its broadcast. Emerging from their squad car were *Adam-12* stars Martin Milner and Kent McCord. The television lawmen flashed smiles at the crowd. Herald Square's lineup included the Rockettes, the Dance Theater of Harlem, and the Broadway cast of *See-Saw*, starring Tommy Tune. Singer Pat Boone replaced Joe Garagiola for the pre-parade show.

Leading the line of march was the Turkey float with country singers George Jones and Tammy Wynette. Parade watchers instantly recognized the Broadway Belle float, which showcased pop stars the Fifth Dimension. Prince Charming was played by television favorite and singer John Davidson.

As the crowds waved to the storybook train, the thunderous roar of a motorcycle engine was heard. Young and old turned their heads, and there before them, with his white helmet and stars-and-stripes jacket, was daredevil stunt cyclist Evel Knievel. The Clydesdale horses again towed the snowman sleigh. Giving these animals some competition were the Lipizzaner horses, a gorgeous assemblage of royal white stallions.

Bullwinkle's foot was punctured during the November 28, 1974, parade. Despite attempts by his handlers to supply air to his brown feet, Bullwinkle had to travel to 34th Street with his injury. Meanwhile, the caterpillar wiggled its way down Broadway. Sunny skies permitted an otherwise trouble-free day for Macy's 48th annual march. A new era would begin with this parade, which included the first appearance of a Sesame Street float featuring characters from the ground-breaking PBS show.

A new float promoted *Planet of the Apes*. The classic 1968 science-fiction thriller was revamped into a short-lived CBS television series starring Roddy McDowall. Paul Lavalle led the All-American Band. Lavalle had become a parade mainstay, providing a decade's worth of holiday music. Also providing hearty Thanksgiving cheer was MGM film musical legend Howard Keel, star of such films as *Seven Brides for Seven Brothers* and *Annie Get Your Gun*, on the festive Turkey float. More music was supplied by the Heywoods on the Disney World Castle float and by the cast of the Broadway smash *Godspell,* who sang on the Circus float. Returning after a long absence was a float devoted to the *Wizard of Oz*, featuring Kathy Colman as Dorothy.

NBC tried out a new anchor lineup for 1974, which included David Hartman (then star of NBC's *Lucas Tanner*), Karen Grassle from *Little House on the Prairie*, and Ed McMahon. Hosting the pre-parade show was Rita Moreno, who starred in PBS's *Electric Company*. Performing before the cameras were Broadway's *The Magic Show* star Doug Henning, the American Ballet Theater, the Spring Branch Bruin Brigade drill team, and, as always, the Rockettes.

NBC brought back Ed McMahon as host on November 27, 1975. Joining McMahon were singer Helen Reddy and *Hollywood Squares* host Peter Marshall. Puppeteer Shari Lewis and her friend Lamb Chop covered the pre-parade activities. The rains pelted the umbrellas, but most of the balloons weathered the storm. Singer Melba Moore rode on the Doodle Bug float, and lighting up the overcast skies with genuine southern hospitality was country music legend Dolly Parton, who was Tom Turkey's passenger. Dolly entertained by singing "Love is Like a Butterfly."

In 1976, the United States proudly celebrated its bicentennial, and the parade celebrated its 50th birthday on November 25. The Macy's event included an astonishing lineup of 400 clowns, 45 floats, 14 bands, and 9 giant balloons. Celebrities appearing were Ed McMahon, making his third NBC broadcast appearance, singer Della Reese, and former *MASH* star McLean Stevenson. Shari Lewis worked a double shift as lead celebrity on the Rocking Horse float. Entertainment for NBC's special Herald Square segment included Metropolitan Opera stars Roberta Peters and Justino Diaz.

Audiences saw the return of television faces from another era, including those of Howdy Doody, Buffalo Bob, and Clarabell the Clown. In contrast, the 49-foot-high Weeble balloon was as unsuccessful this year as it was the previous year in making it to Herald Square. For the 50th time, Santa Claus arrived at Herald Square in his majestic sleigh.

Macy's Golden Anniversary Thanksgiving Day Parade was a resounding success. By 1976, the parade had become a lifetime career for Manfred Bass. His enthusiastic commitment to his job is legendary. When working on a new float inspired by the animated film *Watership Down* for the 1977 parade, Bass traveled to the movie production's British studio to study drawings of the story's rabbits. He also purchased two live rabbits to help him with anatomical perspective. Of course, the two rabbits became a family of many rabbits, and Bass lovingly found a home for each and every one. The dedication to detail paid off, as Bass designed a magnificent float to celebrate his long-eared friends.

Sun broke through cloudy skies on November 24, 1977. Joining Ed McMahon for the NBC telecast were Arte Johnson and singer Carol Lawrence. Broadway's Andrea McArdle of *Annie* helped make Macy's magic on the Big Apple float. Behind the young Broadway actress were the Happy Dragon balloon and the Turkey float, featuring country singer Mel Tillis. Singing star Gloria Gaynor became a Macy's star on the Doodle Bug float. Singer Lou Rawls performed his hit "Lady Love" on the Old Country float. The Tramps rode on the Pirate Ship float, and Neil Sedaka sang his hit "Laughter in the Rain" on the giant Jukebox float.

Cookie mogul Famous Amos rode the Rocking Giraffe just in front of the Mickey Mouse balloon, which cast shadows on spectators cheering from apartment buildings. Before Big Bird and the cast of *Sesame Street* offered Thanksgiving cheer, New Yorkers saw John, Paul, George, and Ringo. The Beatles? Since the real thing was not available, the crowds had to settle for the cast of Broadway's *Beatlemania*. Macy's Parade Studio outdid itself with the creation of the Hobbit float. Based on J. R. R. Tolkien's classic, this float boasted elaborate moving parts and, best of all, a glorious 40-foot dragon with flapping wings. With the fabulous Bugs Bunny follies, Warner Brothers cartoon characters joined the line of march. Raggedy Ann and Andy also skipped about the Midtown pavement. Bands such as Wauwatosa East High School Band, from Wauwatosa, Wisconsin, provided new marching music, including the thunderous theme from *Star Wars*, the movie that was taking America by storm.

New to the parade was Jean McFaddin, who was brought in as producer-director of the parade and annual events. She had a strong professional background in theatrical production and design, along with a boundless amount of enthusiasm for her new role. As a child, she had been entranced as she watched the first national telecast of the parade on NBC from her home in Texas. Now, she found herself producing the amazing event. With Manfred Bass already on board to create new marvels, a truly dynamic duo had teamed up. The vision was clear, McFaddin explained. "The parade is like confetti. It's bright and colorful, with a wonderful sense of movement and surprise. Like confetti, the parade brings out the child in everyone. The goal was—and is—to create that magic each Thanksgiving morning for both the millions of spectators along the parade route and our nationwide television audience." One of the first things McFaddin realized was that "Manny [Bass] needed more time, more support and a real organization behind him. We developed the Parade Studio into an outstanding year-round operation and, with Manny as designer-builder, brought together a phenomenal group of sculptors, welders, painters, and carpenters." Bass found McFaddin's approach innovative, saying that she brought the concept of "theater in the round" to the parade: "The entire parade route—and later, the sky itself—became our stage."

On November 23, 1978, drizzle fell. Joining Ed McMahon was Bryant Gumbel, who was to become host of the *Today Show*. Marching ahead of them were parade veteran Imogene Coca, Broadway's Constance Towers, Tom and Dick Smothers, Ricardo Montalban, Burl Ives, and Yankee baseball star Bucky Dent.

Indiana's Concord Community High School Band gave a dramatic lead-off around 77th Street. The Oak Ridge Boys were the Turkey float's guests. Dancing to the beat on the giant jukebox were the Village People. More music was provided by the Showboat float, which featured Melba Moore, Olympic gold medal winner Bruce Jenner, and actor Peter Ustinov.

Fans of 1950s television cheered at the sight of actors Clayton Moore and Jay Silverheels, better known as the Lone Ranger and Tonto, riding their horses Silver and Scout. Other sights inspired by the world of entertainment included a float featuring figure skater Lynn-Holly Johnson, who was promoting her movie *Ice Castles*; a small-scale log cabin based on the movie the *Wilderness Family, Part 2*; and another float devoted to the Broadway musical *The Wiz*, which was about to be released as a movie. After the success of the previous year's Hobbit float, Macy's returned to the world of J. R. R. Tolkien with a float devoted to the *Lord of the Rings*. The Clydesdale-drawn Loch Ness Monster float was a surefire winner.

Once the pounding drums of the Long Prairie High School Band of Minnesota reached Herald Square, Santa smiled. A new conclusion to the parade was instituted that year. The parade has always included high school marching bands, but this year, for further emphasis, Macy's created a mass band finale to serenade Santa as his sled turned onto 34th Street.

There was no need for Ed McMahon and Bryant Gumbel to don warm overcoats on November 22, 1979. Brilliant sunshine brought warmth to the late-autumn air. Fashion mogul Gloria Vanderbilt was elegant on a wonderfully childlike dollhouse, while game-show host Chuck Woolery took the leash of the Rocking Turtle. With the introduction of what Jean McFaddin calls "toy floats," a new size element was added to the parade. "The scale of Macy's parade is huge!" she exclaims.

As music from the Boardman High School Spartan Marching Band of Youngstown, Ohio, enlivened the 1979 atmosphere, the crowds saw Lionel Hampton and his *Jazz All-Stars* standing with the cast of *Ain't Misbehavin'* on the Showboat float. Down the line was another familiar pop-music stylist, trumpeter Herb Alpert, on the Lunar Moth, a new masterpiece.

The stars were out during daylight. Robert Stack, television's Eliot Ness from *The Untouchables*, joined the parade's family of stars. Comedian and voice actor Larry Storch made friends with the Rocking Horse, and Famous Amos tamed the Rocking Kangaroo. Speaking of kangaroos, sitting on the Circus Wagon was television legend Bob Keeshan, better known as Captain Kangaroo. On Ocean Spray's new Cranberry House float was *Buck Rogers* star Gil Gerard. *Taxi* star Andy Kaufman must have missed his taxi; he arrived late.

Adding to the unpredictability of doing a live broadcast, NBC's telecast was interrupted by special broadcasts reporting that 13 of the Americans being held hostage in Iran had been released. The cutaways featured shots of an empty tarmac in Weisbaden, West Germany, as camera crews anxiously waited to capture the first images of the freed Americans. In her 22-plus years working on the parade, executive producer Jean McFaddin recalls that approximate 17-minute interruption as the only one in parade broadcasts.

In 1980, a returning superhero triumphantly claimed the day for celebrating Americans: Superman was back in the parade. This new version of the Man of Steel featured outstretched arms and a flowing cape. Superman was the 92nd balloon appearing in the parade and the last balloon made by Goodyear. Only a superman could handle 12,000 cubic feet of helium.

For star quality, the Pirate Ship float featured the cast of the musical *The Pirates of Penzance*. People with cameras snapped shots of rock star Linda Ronstadt, singer Rex Smith, actor George Rose, and rising star Kevin Kline. On the Showboat float was Broadway dynamo Chita Rivera. Danielle Brisebois, the newest cast member from *All in the Family*, rode on Ocean Spray's Cranberry House float. Next in line were Stephanie Mills, Broadway's Dorothy from *The Wiz*, on the Rocking Lion, and pop stars the Captain and Tennille in the dollhouse.

The worlds of *Sesame Street* and Walt Disney held their usual places in the line of march. The castle float promoted Disney's rereleased animated hit feature *Aristocats*. A new float for 1980 was devoted to the upcoming *Legend of the Lone Ranger* movie and featured a stagecoach.

It was Ohio's Warren Junior Military Academy Marching Band that ushered in Santa Claus for Thanksgiving 1980. NBC's telecast was a family tradition with ever-growing ratings. It was evident when the parade stopped in front of the cameras in Herald Square that the best was yet to come.

A new Mickey Mouse balloon takes a test flight in 1971, 27 years after his first parade appearance. (Courtesy of Engineered Fabrics.)

Along with Smokey the Bear, Mickey Mouse finally got his chance to march down the route in 1972; weather conditions the previous year had kept the giant balloons out of the parade. Underdog and the rest of the favorites from the Goodyear warehouse triumphantly returned to the parade. Only Donald Duck was injured, puncturing his hand. Sadly, parade officials announced that this would be the duck's last appearance for a while. (Courtesy of *New York Daily News*.)

In 1973, the parade celebrated the 50th anniversary of Walt Disney cartoons with many of Disney's famous cartoon figures. Balloons given flight tickets were Bullwinkle, Linus the Lionhearted, the Happy Dragon, Smokey the Bear, Underdog, Dino the Dinosaur, Snoopy, and, of course, Mickey Mouse. In keeping with Disney's 50th anniversary, the family entertainment giant was well represented. Mickey, Pluto, and Goofy could be seen near Disney's Circus Wagon float. Other Disney floats were the Alice in Wonderland float, Captain Hook's ship, and the Disney World Castle, which that year showcased the studio's new animated feature *Robin Hood*. Disney and company marched in step with heroically named bands, including the Wrangler Belles of Cisco, Texas, and the Mohawk Musical Corps of Garretsville, Ohio. (Courtesy of *New York Daily News*.)

Just "bearly" eight years old, the Smokey the Bear balloon was already a big star in 1974. (Courtesy of Bill Smith collection.)

Like Smokey the Bear and these smiling clowns, the merrymakers marched to 34th Street in 1976. The Shaggy Dog joined Pluto and Goofy on the Disney wagon, while Snow White, the Seven Dwarfs, and Peter Pan made Mouseketeers proud. In 1976, the venerable shoe float had an added surprise. Singing "The Sunny Side of the Street" was famed comedienne Martha Raye. (Courtesy of *New York Daily News*.)

An example of parade designers breaking new ground was 1975's giant Cootie Bug. For years, floats had been basically rectangular platforms, but here was an actual reproduction of the toy, with a body consisting of huge spheres and legs extending outward and downward. On the Cootie Bug float was the little red-headed television-commercial sensation, Mason Reese. After many parade appearances, the popular Cootie Bug was retired and donated to a children's museum in Washington, D.C. The Sesame Street float returned, along with Disney favorites the castle float, Captain Hook's ship, and the carnival-like Disney wagon. Illusionist Doug Henning cast his magical spell on the Wizard of Oz float. Among the new floats braving wet streets was a special one devoted to America's upcoming 1976 bicentennial celebration. Macy's workers dressed in 18th-century fashions rode the Old Country float, which was brimming with period flavor and pulled by the Clydesdales. (Courtesy of *New York Daily News*.)

Two well-known employees from Milwaukee's Shotz Brewery were thrust into the holiday spotlight in 1976. Enter Laverne and Shirley, also known as Penny Marshall and Cindy Williams, the stars of the smash television series. Providing a spectacular parade performance, singer Barry Manilow sang his hit "It's a Miracle," which fit the occasion. More music was provided by tunesmith Paul Williams and the cast of the kids-as-gangsters movie *Bugsy Malone*. (Courtesy of *New York Daily News*.)

Making his debut in 1977 was *Sesame Street*'s Kermit the Frog balloon, who in his puppet size was voiced by Muppet creator Jim Henson. Kermit took his place alongside his balloon friends. There was good news that year, as the Weeble balloon made its first appearance in Herald Square. (Courtesy of Goodyear Tire and Rubber Company collection, the University of Akron Archives.)

Kermit the Frog returned in 1978 for his second flight, as did Snoopy the Aviator. The usual difficulty in handling the giant balloons on rainy Thanksgivings yielded one casualty: the Happy Dragon. The veteran was punctured after doing battle with a tree in Columbus Circle. To the delight of everyone, the rain just seemed to bounce off the balloon friends. (Courtesy of Lockheed Martin, Akron.)

"Speed of lighting, roar of thunder!" Underdog is seen here at the 1978 parade. (Courtesy of Bill Smith collection.)

Mickey Mouse again proved popular in the 1978 parade. (Courtesy of Lockheed Martin, Akron.)

NBC ensured that a feast of celebrities took part in the holiday festivities. In 1979, Buddy Hackett provided color, and Erik Estrada of *C.H.I.P.S.* upheld law and order. Actress Sandy Duncan portrayed Peter Pan. Leading the march was the Tom Turkey float with Mickey Rooney, followed by tap-dancer and Broadway's *Sugarbabies* star Ann Miller, who gave her feet a rest by riding in a horse-drawn carriage. (Courtesy of Macy's.)

Enthroned on the *New York Daily News*'s Big Apple float in 1979 was bona fide pop royalty. Looking radiant atop an oversized apple and wearing bright green furs was legend Diana Ross. (Courtesy of *New York Daily News*.)

Roving *New York Daily News* photographers chronicled a collage of happy faces on Thanksgiving Day in 1979. Joyful children sat on their fathers' shoulders, mischievous lads perched atop sidewalk traffic signs, and apartment dwellers cheered from their balconies. (Courtesy of *New York Daily News*.)

In 1979, with the *Sesame Street* gang's popularity growing, Macy's expanded the Muppet–filled float to include a mobile sight called the Electric Mayhem Bus. It featured Kermit's girlfriend Miss Piggy and, of course, Jim Henson. (Courtesy of *New York Daily News*.)

This artist is working faster than a snail's pace in this 1980 photograph. (Courtesy of *New York Daily News*.)

Be a clown! Be a clown! This photograph was taken in 1980. (Courtesy of *New York Daily News*.)

Here comes Sister Sledge on the Turkey float in 1980. (Photograph by Bill Smith.)

The Spinners ride on the Lunar Moth float in 1980. (Photograph by Bill Smith.)

The balloon contingent in 1981 totaled nine and included Snoopy, who, having been deflated in the 1980 parade, sported a visible scar. Also in the parade were Kermit the Frog, Superman, and Mickey Mouse. With the aid of hot cocoa (savvy paradegoers brought their own supply), pretzels, and chestnuts to warm their bodies, the spectators waited for the arrival of Santa Claus to warm their hearts. (Courtesy of Bill Smith collection.)

Celebrities in the 1982 parade included Mr. Television, veteran parade personality Milton Berle (pictured here), and the legendary Sammy Davis Jr. (Courtesy of *New York Daily News*.)

*Seven*

# THE 1980S

# BALLOONS! OLD FAVORITES AND

# NEW WONDERS

The 1980s began with the end of the Iranian hostage crisis on January 20, 1981, coinciding with Ronald Reagan's inauguration as the 40th president of the United States. Throughout the decade, the economy boomed as America spent, spent, and spent. Then, on January 28, 1986, tragedy struck. The space shuttle *Challenger* exploded, taking the lives of seven astronauts, as the nation watched. As the decade came to a close, communism took a hit on November 9, 1989, when the demolition of the Berlin Wall began; the wall had been a symbol of oppression and the division between the East and the West since 1961.

Throughout all of this change, Americans tuned in every Thanksgiving to see new balloon wonders take their places in the Macy's Thanksgiving Day Parade. Macy's entered the decade with the 55th edition of the parade on November 26, 1981. Featured in the advertisements were balloon veterans Bullwinkle, making his 21st parade appearance, and Underdog, making his 17th appearance. They were truly the stars of the parade. Despite the 30-degree temperatures, more than a million people lined the parade route, and an estimated 80 million tuned into the parade via television.

The 1981 parade included 13 marching bands from as far away as Homewood, Alabama (represented by the Homewood Patriot band) and California. Among the 18 floats, a favorite was the Big Apple float, sponsored by the *New York Daily News,* with baseball player Dave Winfield of the New York Yankees waving to fans from the top. This float, portraying the New York skyline, quickly became a hometown hit. Other personalities included Phyllis Diller as Cinderella and *C.H.I.P.S.* star Erik Estrada as Prince Charming. Estrada had appeared previously in the parade, and Diller made the trip down Broadway again in 1986. For the 56th edition on November 25, 1982, two new balloons rose to the occasion: Olive Oyl and Woody Woodpecker. Atop the Big Apple float, Sammy Davis Jr. sang his hit "The Candy Man."

The stunning advertisement of Sunday, November 20, 1983, trumpeted the 57th edition of the parade. The advertisement featured Underdog, Woody Woodpecker, Yogi Bear, and Bullwinkle. Once the first units of the procession had passed, Macy's 9 balloons, 17 floats, and 12 marching bands followed. Escorting the floats and filling in gaps between the balloons were thousands of Macy's volunteers dressed as clowns. Batman and Wonder Woman walked along the streets; crime fighting had to wait until after the parade was over. Country singer Charley Pride sat upon the Turkey float, and as it stopped in front of Macy's, Pride sang a song. Other celebrities included Miss America Vanessa Williams on the Big Apple float.

Right behind Santa in popularity were the Muppets. Jim Henson's newest curious creations, the Fraggles of *Fraggle Rock,* had their own float and performed the theme from their Home Box Office (HBO) series. Also singing for the spectators was the Boys Choir of Harlem. The Radio City Rockettes did their precision dancing, making way for Santa's entrance. Cloudy skies had threatened from early dawn and drizzle broke out, but an estimated crowd of 750,000 attended the event.

The advertisement appearing in newspapers on Wednesday, November 21, 1984, was one of the most visually attractive of the 1980s. According to Jean McFaddin, "the balloon inflation became an event within the event. The growing crowds soon realized it has a magic all its own." McFaddin stated, "We were looking to create flying scenes." In future years, there would be Betty Boop flying on the moon, Bart Simpson soaring down Broadway on a giant skateboard, and the *Rugrats'* Chuckie and Tommy catching a ride down the parade route aboard their pet dog, Spike.

Parade day on November 22, 1984, was cold, but the crowds easily numbered a million, packing streets and curbsides 10 deep along the route. The parade featured the debuts of Raggedy Ann and Garfield, and old favorite Donald Duck, after years in the Macy's warehouse, took another flight down the route in honor of his 50th birthday.

Before the parade reached 34th Street, viewers in Herald Square and at home watched Jacques d'Amboise's National Dance Institute (a group of city youths) and singer Maureen McGovern perform. They also watched Hinton Battle dance, heard Menudo sing (to avoid a riot, the group was kept under wraps, waiting at the store loading dock), and saw the Mocko Jumbi Dancers perform.

Once the kickoff band passed in front of Macy's, Bryant Gumbel, Pat Sajak from *Wheel of Fortune,* and Stephanie Kramer of *Hunter* provided color commentary. Florence Henderson, who played Carol Brady on *The Brady Bunch,* appeared as a special guest host. The Turkey float brought returning parade star Dionne Warwick before the crowds. Opera star Placido Domingo dreamt of a white Christmas from the Big Apple float, and actor Robert Vaughn gave tribute to the Statue of Liberty aboard the Macy's clipper. Bob McGrath and his friends from *Sesame Street* delighted the children. Comic Tim Conway performed with the Cabbage Patch Kids, and television star Kaye Ballard sang "Home for the Holidays." Afterward, Santa arrived in Herald Square, concluding another grand parade.

The 1985 advertisement continued the less-is-more trend and showcased the giant balloons. On November 28, 1985, due to rain, the balloons encountered the roughest going in years. Superman (who tore his leg), Kermit the Frog (who ripped his stomach along Central Park West), and their fellow giants may have felt a little down, but they were not out, as their balloon handlers safely guided (and sometimes carried) them across the finish line. A triumphant, 72-foot-tall Betty Boop stayed upon her moon and quickly won over the crowd. Providing color for the telecast were Pat Sajak, Bert Convey, and *The Cosby Show*'s Phylicia Ayers-Allen-Rashad, whose television children also appeared in that year's march. The rain gave Don Correia's performance of "Singin' in the Rain" from the Broadway show a touch of reality. The cast of Broadway's *The Mystery of Edwin Drood*—Betty Buckley, George Rose, and Cleo Lane—also performed. The Concorde Community High School Band of Elkhart, Indiana, kicked off the parade.

As always, the parade that year included featured a variety of celebrities along with the floats and balloons. Musical group Woody Herman and the Young Thundering Herd rode on the Herald Square Express. On Macy's paddle wheeler, performers from the Broadway show *Big River* entertained. On the Care Bear float, Miss America Susan Akin entertained. Pop group New Edition and *Miami Vice*'s Philip Michael Thomas also performed. Garfield and Snoopy the Aviator led the way for Betty Boop. The seaworthy Macy's clipper had clear sailing, and country singer Lee Greenwood sang "God Bless the USA" with the original torch of the Statue of Liberty right behind him. Aboard Macy's Boyertown trolley, singer Tony Bennett crooned "I Left My Heart in San Francisco." Pop star Shannon sang "Let the Music Play" while rocking on the Rocking Horse. Film and recording star Rosemary Clooney offered a classy rendition of "White Christmas." It was another successful year.

The advertisement on Sunday, November 23, 1986 offered a lot to anticipate. Forecasts called for temperatures in the upper 40s to low 50s and sunny skies. Game show host Pat Sajak and television celebrity Stephanie Kramer gave the commentary. Featured in the telecast and performing before the parade reached Macy's were multitalented Nell Carter of *Gimme a Break,* parade veterans the Mocko Jumbi Dancers, dancer Ann Reinking (who was appearing in a revival of *Sweet Charity*), and *Barney Miller* star Hal Linden. The first band was also a parade veteran, the

Homewood Patriot Band of Homewood, Alabama. The Turkey float gave country star Crystal Gayle a grand ride, and she returned the favor by singing "Winter Wonderland."

Actor Robert Vaughn made another parade appearance and recited the preamble to the Constitution. Opera star Robert Merrill sang from the Macy's clipper; there were no choppy seas. Film star Dolph Lundgren of *Rocky IV* narrated a set piece hyping the film *Masters of the Universe.* Adding to the family fun were comedienne Phyllis Diller, this time as Mother Goose, and actress Celeste Holm, riding in Cinderella's regal carriage. Musical group Sawyer Brown took to the rails on the Herald Square Express.

Olive Oyl carried Swee' Pee on her arm; behind her, country-singing legend Dottie West made sure she took the first stagecoach to Macy's. In the cockpit of Macy's flyer, the "King of the Road" himself, singer-songwriter Roger Miller, sang a song from Broadway's *Big River.* Actress and singer Shirley Jones had the circus wagon take her past Macy's, stopping long enough to sing. The Rockettes performed before Santa arrived to finish the parade. With sunny skies but tricky winds, the balloons had a rough time navigating the route. Superman lost his left hand at 77th Street. The Raggedy Ann balloon triumphed over a street lamp. Olive Oyl and Garfield also encountered—and overcame—their own share of difficulties.

The weather for the 1987 parade, held on November 26, was a virtual carbon copy of the previous year's. The estimated 2.1 million people crowding the route witnessed new balloons take to the skies. Kermit was there, along with newcomers Snuggle the Bear, Ronald McDonald, and Snoopy on Skates—the best Snoopy to date, sporting a Macy's ski sweater. With the creative and technological advancements of each new helium giant, Macy's continued to raise the ooh–and–ahh level of spectators young and old.

That year, the balloon lineup numbered 10. Uptown, the balloons waited to take their positions in the line of march. Downtown, Joel Grey performed a number from the revival of *Cabaret,* followed by a presentation of songs from *Les Miserables.* As the Albertville High School Marching Band of Albertville, Indiana, entered the concrete canyon, the parade followed in strong fashion. From the Turkey float, Rita Coolidge sang "Your Love Is Lifting Me Higher." Parade emcee of 1950, Bert Parks, sang the praises of the family dog aboard the Great American Dog float. On the Strawberry Cottage float, country-singing sensations the Oak Ridge Boys sang "Hear My Heart Beat." Television pioneer and parade veteran Buffalo Bob Smith was joined by Clarabell the Clown and Howdy Doody on the Carson City Stagecoach. During the telecast, Muppet creator Jim Henson was presented with the Rollie Award (named after R. H. Macy) for the 11 years of Muppet participation in the parade.

In a charming number, singer Bobby Vinton performed "Santa Must Be Polish" while folk dancers danced around the Macy's flyer he piloted. "The Penguin Hop" was performed by Judy Kaye and penguin-costumed dancers aboard a winter-themed float. Championship ice-skater Jill Schultz, daughter of *Peanuts* creator Charles Schultz, skated around a float, preparing the way for the Snoopy on Skates balloon. Before Santa arrived, Snuggle the Bear, in a huge Christmas stocking, took his first trip into Herald Square.

Advertisements proclaiming "It's Macy's 62nd Annual Thanksgiving Day Parade" worked like a charm. A record three million people turned out on November 24, 1988. Willard Scott was joined by co-host and parade veteran Sandy Duncan. The balloon platoon numbered 10 for the second year in a row. Making his debut was the Nestle Quik bunny, who quickly became a Macy's star.

The 1988 event featured a great mix of entertainment. On the Turkey float, which was making its 17th trip, was country singer Tanya Tucker. Frankie Valli of *Four Seasons* fame sang his hit "Grease" from atop the Strawberry Cottage float. Opera singer Marilyn Horne was on the Statue of Liberty float. Performer Peter Allen performed a song from the show *Legs Diamond* while steaming down to Herald Square on the Herald Square Express. Motown legends the Four Tops took the Big Apple float on a trip while performing for the crowds. Animation legend Friz Freleng rode down the route, ushering in his creation the Pink Panther. By 11:40 a.m., the Rockettes performed, and the crowds got the chance to welcome Santa.

The advertisement appearing in newspapers on Sunday, November 19, 1989, was the least detailed in the parade's history. Featuring Art Deco style, the advertisement promoted the new balloons Bugs Bunny and Big Bird. Yet the parade that year was truly memorable. The day before the 63rd edition, Wednesday, November 22, 1989, had the weathermen checking their charts and computer printouts; snow was in the forecast. With the temperature reaching 40 degrees on Wednesday, no one thought an accumulation would be possible. The first flakes started falling about 10:30 p.m. By 2:00 a.m. on Thanksgiving morning, November 23, 1989, two inches had fallen. With temperatures in the upper 20s, the snow piled up to nearly six inches across the metropolitan area.

The weather kept Bugs Bunny from making his debut, and Snoopy was grounded. However, the Quik bunny, Big Bird, Spiderman, Ronald McDonald, the Pink Panther, and Woody Woodpecker had fun frolicking in the flurries. Teen pop group the New Kids on the Block rode the Big Apple float. The Nitty Gritty Dirt Band, Melba Moore, and, atop the Turkey float, country star Clint Black, all entertained. Even with the persistent flurries and biting cold, 1.8 million people gathered along the route.

Bands supplied Christmas carols as they marched, completing the Currier and Ives pictures of the city. The bands from Hawaii and Florida probably got over the novelty of the snow rather quickly and wished for the sunnier and warmer locales of their homes. Paradegoers and television watchers enjoyed the show unaware of the spirit shown by parade participants and parade organizers behind the scenes. One particularly dedicated parade clown captain brought a group of clown volunteers from the Macy's store in Albany, New York. Jean McFaddin vividly remembers the group: "The buses couldn't get through to many of our branch store groups because of the snow, and Albany was no exception. With no bus in sight, at three o'clock in the morning, our Albany clown captain took all of his recruits to the train station and, with his own credit card, bought tickets for the 30 employees. They rode the train all night to Grand Central Station. Arriving in Manhattan, they couldn't get crosstown transportation, so they proceeded to walk 10 blocks or so through the snow to Herald Square, where they put on their clown costumes. And, thanks to their captain, they marched happily in the parade."

Buses were not the only thing in short supply. Due to the snowstorm, many of the balloon handlers were not going to make it to the parade. At 2:30 a.m., McFaddin called Mike Miller, who organizes the huge group of young cheerleaders that annually appears in the parade, asking for his help. Miller quickly responded by getting his 1,000 cheerleaders to the starting line immediately to help supplement the balloon handler program. After a wintry 2.5 miles, the cheerleaders were exhausted, but they went on to perform a great production number for the NBC telecast. The spirit and perseverance of all participating Macy's employees and volunteers made the parade what the millions of spectators were eagerly anticipating on the unforgettable November morning.

The 1990 advertisement was eye candy. An estimated 2.2 million spectators turned out for the event. Back again as co-hosts for the telecast were Willard Scott, whose genuine love for the event was evident, and Deborah Norville. The balmy breezes brushed aside the chill. Clifford the Big Red Dog proved he was top dog upon his debut this year; joining him in debuting this year was Bart Simpson. All the balloons flew in front of Macy's in fine form.

After being entertained by Olympic gold medalist Cathy Rigby, who performed a number from the show *Peter Pan,* paradegoers rocked along to music from Broadway's *Buddy: The Buddy Holly Story* and enjoyed numbers from *Forever Plaid* and *Nunsense*. The crowds could see the parade heading their way. Country music's Garth Brooks was joined by his wife, Sandy, atop the Turkey float as he sang "Two of a Kind, Working on a Full House." From the Indian Canoe float, Patti Labelle sang "Wouldn't It Be Beautiful." Judy Kaye rode on another standout float, entitled Heroes of Our Frontier Past, which featured larger-than-life depictions of folk heroes Paul Bunyan, John Henry, and Pecos Bill. Singer Barry Manilow made another appearance in this year's parade as well.

The balloons had a difficult time navigating the city streets in 1982. Bullwinkle (or Bull*wrinkle*) sprang a leak and was escorted out of the parade at 37th Street. Woody Woodpecker suffered a couple of punctures but did manage to fly past Macy's. Snoopy's tail deflated. Superman, Linus the Lionhearted, Kermit the Frog, and Mickey Mouse faced turbulence but endured. (Courtesy of Macy's.)

Don't miss a moment of it! The stars! The balloons! The floats, old and new! And of course, the arrival of Santa himself. It all marks the official start of a New York Christmas. There's just nothing else like it, and it's all in the spirit of giving. 9 am sharp, Thanksgiving morning, November 25th, at Central Park West and 77th Street, all the way down to Herald Square (and into the hearts of millions). For up-to-the-minute Parade information, call our special hotline number (212) 560-4495.

Come share it all. See it live or on
NBC-TV, 9 am to 12 noon.

In 1982, Olive Oyl had the honor of being one of the first female balloons in the parade (Mrs. Katzenjammer of the 1920s was the first). Walter Lantz's Woody Woodpecker, debuting as a balloon that year, gained a whole new generation of fans through his parade appearances. (Courtesy of *New York Daily News*.)

133

Lights! Camera! Woody! As the parade marched toward Herald Square in 1983, television cameras focused on Woody Woodpecker as well as on Broadway stars Tommy Tune and Twiggy, who were performing a number from *My One and Only.* (Photograph by Bill Smith.)

Macy's Jean McFaddin is seen here with her pal Snoopy in 1983. Macy's giant balloons had entered a period of transition, to be completed over three years. Goodyear Rubber and Tire Company officials felt that they could no longer take the time to manufacture one-of-a-kind balloons, nor could they provide the annual maintenance they required. Therefore, Macy's turned to a smaller balloon-manufacturing company, Kemp Balloons, which provided the necessary support for the next two years. (Courtesy of *New York Daily News.*)

Yogi had a grand time as he soared above the street in 1983. Olive Oyl took her second stroll down the route. Joining her was Woody Woodpecker. The balloons became bigger stars as crowds gathered in greater numbers on the eve of the parade to watch the balloons take shape. It was Macy's magic. (Courtesy of *New York Daily News*.)

Underdog encountered turbulence on 51st Street in 1984, but he quickly took to the air again after a brief dive. Woody Woodpecker got snagged in the trees and flew low at 77th Street to get a gander at the crowds, but he took to the skies for the rest of the trek. (Photograph by Bill Smith.)

Without a "pic-a-nic" basket, Yogi is still all smiles as he passes Macy's in 1984. (Photograph by Bill Smith.)

OSCAR MAYERS

This 1984 sketch captures the right spirit of the Statue of Liberty. The float became a standout. (Courtesy of Macy's, illustration by Manfred Bass.)

The Quik bunny "quikly" became a parade superstar in 1986. Another special highlight of the 60th-anniversary festivities was Humpty Dumpty, who took to the skies as the 100th giant character balloon; later, he was transformed into a "falloon," a combination of a float and a balloon. (Courtesy of Macy's. Illustration by Manfred Bass.)

Wow, bow wow! Toby is fetching in 1987. (Courtesy of *New York Daily News*.)

With the 1990 parade, Macy's introduced a new word into parade vocabulary: "falloon," a combination float and balloon. The concept was an instant hit thanks to the Wizard of Oz falloon, which depicted the Wicked Witch gazing into her crystal ball at a magical vision of the famous foursome: Dorothy, the Scarecrow, the Tin Man, and the Cowardly Lion. Paddington Bear was the second falloon. Pointing out why the falloon concept is important to the parade, Jean McFaddin said, "It allows us to incorporate the magic of balloon with the theatrical, storylike environment of the float. It adds yet another scale and sense of wonder to the parade." This year was also special for Daniel Frey, who was a volunteer in Macy's first parade in 1924. He rode along the route in a parade vehicle. He, like the countless other thousands of Macy's volunteers that have made this event possible, deserve the nation's heartfelt thanks. (Courtesy of Macy's.)

*Eight*

# THE 1990S

## GLORIOUS BALLOONS!

## BIGGER AND BIGGER!

As the 1990s began, so did Operation Desert Storm. Thankfully, the confrontation was not a prolonged one. Bill Clinton became the 42nd president of the United States. By the mid-1990s, the country was on the road back to economic health. As the Macy's Thanksgiving Day Parade entered the 1990s, the event continued to get better.

In the 1990s, every facet of the parade, from print advertisements to television coverage, became glossier; yet the event retained its special mix of fantasy, spectacle, and wonder.

In 1991, the parade celebrated its 65th anniversary, and NBC celebrated its 40th telecast of the parade. Stage, screen, and music were represented. Opera star Kathleen Battle sang from the Indian Canoe float, the country band the Kentucky Headhunters performed the theme from *Davy Crockett* aboard the Heroes of the American Frontier float, and country star Charlie Daniels entertained from the Turkey float. Aboard the Herald Square Express, brothers Andy, Matthew, and Joey Lawrence waved to their fans along the route. The cast of the film update of *The Addams Family* passed by Macy's. Sports stars Joe Peppitone and Ron Greschner joined entertainer Ben Vereen on the Big Apple float. On a huge baseball glove, rhythm-and-blues sensations Boyz II Men sang "Motown Philly." Powerhouse singer Jennifer Holiday of Broadway's *Dreamgirls* gave a riveting performance from the Statue of Liberty float.

Newcomer Babar the Elephant made an appearance, and old favorites Linus the Lionhearted (who was 65 feet long and filled with 9,000 cubic feet of helium) and the Happy Dragon were welcomed back from retirement. Deflation may have had Kermit and Betty Boop under the weather, but Spiderman (with 8,300 cubic feet of helium), Woodstock, Woody Woodpecker (making his ninth flight), and the rest of Macy's balloon stars all rose to the occasion.

On November 25, 1992, the new balloon on the block was Goofy, a film star since 1932. Wearing a Santa suit and flying in an animated pose, the Goofy balloon captured the Disney character's personality. Rain failed to dampen the holiday spirit; an estimated two million spectators lined the route. Before the parade entered Herald Square, casts from *Jelly's Last Jam, Guys and Dolls, Crazy for You, Five Guys Named Moe,* and *Falsetto's* gave their all for the crowds.

At 10:00 a.m., with the West Orange High School Band of Winter Garden, Florida, sounding the first musical notes, the parade passed in front of Herald Square. Country singer Mac Davis (having replaced Keith Carradine in *The Will Rogers Follies)* was in tune on the Turkey float. Country singers McBride and the Ride rode to Macy's on the Western Town float. From atop the Big Apple float, rhythm-and-blues singer Shanice sang "I Love Your Smile" to boxing champion Riddick Bowe. Opera great Jessye Norman had the honor of taking Miss Liberty down Broadway. Comic Cheech Marin sang about his job as the "Yellow School Bus Driver." The Stars on Parade float came down the route with Miss America Leanza Cornett. Country singer Aaron Tippen sang "I Wouldn't Have It Any Other Way." Performing "A Whole New World," from Disney's animated gem *Aladdin,* were Peabo Bryson and Regina Belle.

In 1993, Macy's once again premiered four balloons: the canine star Beethoven, the 1996

Olympic games mascot Izzy, video-game icon Sonic the Hedgehog, and the dinosaur from the animated film *We're Back,* Rex. Winds added to the chill of the 30-degree temperatures and resulted in some balloon mishaps: at 58th Street, Sonic the Hedgehog struck a lamppost and deflated, missing his debut at Macy's; Bart Simpson got a gash in his back but managed to finish the two-mile trek. Smokey the Bear was reinflated for the first time since 1981 in honor of his 50th birthday. Broadway shows *Joseph and the Amazing Technicolor Dreamcoat, She Loves Me, Tommy,* and the revival of *My Fair Lady* held the spotlight before the parade arrived at Macy's. Dave Thomas of Wendy's hamburger fame rode aboard the Home for the Holidays float, and superstar Stevie Wonder performed "Take Time Out" on the Cornucopia float. Other celebrities included Dirk Blocker and Michael Landon Jr. (sons of television's Cartwrights Dan Blocker and Michael Landon) portraying Cartwrights on the Western Town float. Film star Debbie Reynolds's rendition of the song "Good Morning" was a highlight for fans of the movie *Singin' in the Rain.* Reynolds performed on the American Movie Classics Hollywood Express Train, which also carried film star Eva Marie Saint and the channel's host, Bob Dorian.

From television's groundbreaking show of the 1960s, *Laugh-In,* Joanne Worley and Ruth Buzzy inhabited the Wonderful World of Mother Goose float, and Lorenzo Lamas, son of movie star Fernando Lamas, stood bravely on the Dragon Tales float.

The 27-degree temperature on November 24, 1994, put a chill in the air for the parade. Bob and Dolores Hope, enclosed in a plastic box, rode on the Statue of Liberty float; parade officials stressed that the box was to ward off the chill. Wendy's Christmas Tree float carried film star Connie Stevens, and her daughters Tricia Leigh Fisher and Joley Fisher gave the crowd a happy holiday helping of "Jingle Bell Rock" and "Rocking around the Christmas Tree." From the circus wagon, Natalie Cole sang a smooth "No More Blue Christmas." On the Cornucopia float, legendary performer Judy Collins returned to the parade. Kenny G, on the Humpty Dumpty falloon, continued the easy listening with his rendition of "Winter Wonderland." The *New York Daily News*'s Big Apple float carried wrestling star Lex Luger.

November 23, 1995, was gray and windy with temperatures in the 30s. Matthew Broderick from *How to Succeed in Business Without Really Trying,* legendary Carol Channing and the cast of *Hello Dolly* (which was enjoying a revival), and the cast of *Smokey Joe's Café* gave their all before the parade arrived. The honor of kicking off the parade again went to the Homewood Patriot High School Band of Homewood, Alabama. Other bands came from Ohio, Mississippi, and Nebraska, among other states. Other celebrities included rap artist LL Cool J, singer Jon Secada, Ben Vereen, Ann B. Davis (who played Alice on *The Brady Bunch*), Kelsey Grammer of *Frasier,* parade veteran Shari Lewis and her furry friends, and new singing sensations All 4-One.

The weather challenged the balloon handlers. Sonic the Hedgehog missed his moment in Herald Square, but Sky Dancer and the Pink Panther reached the finish line, along with most of their fellow balloons. Balloon veteran Garfield hit a lamppost at 52nd Street but bounced back in fine form to finish the route.

The 1996 edition celebrated a milestone: the 70th anniversary of the parade. In honor of the anniversary, Macy's presented another Bullwinkle—not the classic balloon of 1961 but a new design that included his trusty friend Rocket J. Squirrel, known as "Rocky." The show-stopping Broadway performances that year included Bebe Nuewirth's dazzling "All That Jazz" from *Chicago,* followed by Savion Glover and crew's rapid-fire dancing from *Bring in 'Da Noise, Bring in 'Da Funk,* and Tony-winning Donna Murphy and the children from the *King and I* singing "Getting to Know You." One of the best highlights in all the years of parade coverage was presented by the cast of *Rent,* who sang "Seasons of Love."

The Turkey float carried rock-and-roll legend Bo Diddley. After Bullwinkle made his long-awaited return, wearing a beanie and a Wossa Motta U sweater, the 68-foot-tall moose made way for the M&M Chocolate Colorworks falloon, with the Lawrence brothers aboard. Next was Garfield. The Big Bird balloon followed the cast of *Sesame Street.* To the delight of parade fans, Macy's revived two balloon classics from the 1940s: the 30-foot-long flying fish and Harold the Fireman. Parade veteran Shirley Jones rode on the American Movie Classics float, and Vanessa

Williams returned to the parade. Also returning were the Captain and Tennille, who sang "Love Will Keep Us Together" on the Dunkin' Donuts float. Shari Lewis, on the Herald Square Express, traveled the route, followed by Kenny Rogers on the spectacular Snow Family float. As always, Santa signaled the arrival of the Christmas season.

The glorious advertisement for the 71st Macy's Thanksgiving Day Parade featured balloons as far as the eye could see. Macy's introduced four new balloons for the 1997 edition: the Rugrats, featuring characters from the popular animated show on Nickelodeon; Bumpé the Laplandic Cow; Arthur the Aardvark, from the PBS children's series; and Petula the Pig, a Macy's original character. Preparations were under way, but there were concerns on the weather front. High winds were forecasted for Thanksgiving Eve and Thanksgiving Day.

On November 27, Thanksgiving Day, weatherman Al Roker and Macy's Jean McFaddin cut the ribbon and proclaimed "Let's have a parade!" The colorful holiday treat marched smartly toward Herald Square. Hosting chores for NBC went to Willard Scott and Katie Couric. *Chicago* was a hit in New York, thanks to the jazzy Roaring Twenties–style "Press Conference Rag," which was performed by stars Marilu Henner and James McNaughton. Other highlights included the Backstreet Boys performing "As Long As You Love Me" aboard the You Can See the Future float and country royalty Wynonna singing "Change the World" aboard the Statue of Liberty float. The Macy's clipper was rechristened Peter Pan's Pirate Ship in honor of its passenger, Peter Pan, played by Cathy Rigby, who performed "Never Never Land." Another crowd favorite was television's Hal Linden riding on the Alice in Wonderland float. The former Barney Miller was not pounding the beat but rehearsing his "bah humbugs" in preparation for his portrayal of Scrooge in a new holiday tradition, *A Christmas Carol* at the Paramount Theatre.

Experiencing the thrill of appearing in its first Macy's Thanksgiving Day Parade was the Trumbull High School Band of Trumbull, Connecticut, accompanied by parade veterans the Concord High School Band of Elkhart, Indiana, and the Allen High School Band of Texas. Wrapping up the parade were Vicki Lewis singing "Join the Circus" atop the Circus float, musician John Tesh, Mary Kate and Ashley Olsen, Toby the Parade Dog (a mechanical pooch), the Clydesdale horses, and the Anastasia float.

The highflying heroes were buffeted by high winds in what proved to be their roughest trek since 1971. Newcomers Bumpé the Laplandic Cow, the Rugrats, and Arthur the Aardvark made a triumphant journey into Herald Square. The other newcomer, Petula the Pig, decided to sit the day out to debut another year. As in the previous 70 parades, Santa brought up the rear. Weather reports Thanksgiving morning had indicated that the rough weather had subsided. While the parade was in full swing, the winds picked up again. Caught by a gust of wind, one of the balloons knocked into a street lamp, causing injury to a parade spectator. In the parade's long history, Macy's has always put great emphasis on the safety of spectators and participants alike. Macy's and the city of New York acted swiftly to create specific regulations for the flying of the parade balloons, ensuring that the Macy's Thanksgiving Day Parade would continue to enchant everyone, everywhere.

On November 14, 1998, with the 72nd edition of the big parade just around the corner, Macy's premiered two of three new giant balloons at Stevens Institute in Hoboken, New Jersey. Babe the Pig, at nearly 37 feet tall, 28 feet wide, and 60 feet long, was every bit as cute and cuddly as his movie counterpart. Dexter, the title character from *Dexter's Laboratory,* was some 57 feet high and had a jet pack on his back. The Wild Thing, familiar to children everywhere, unfortunately had to delay his debut.

Forecasts predicted rain on November 26, 1998, and the day was indeed wet and wild. After the great opening by America Sings!, hosts Katie Couric, Matt Lauer, and Al Roker introduced performances from Broadway's *Footloose, Cabaret, The Scarlett Pimpernel,* and the upcoming *Annie Get Your Gun.*

At 10:00 a.m., the parade was escorted into Herald Square by a motorcycle brigade of New York City highway patrolmen, making way for the highflying Cloe the Clown balloon. The Franklin High School marching band of Franklin, Tennessee, passed by the reviewing stand to the tune of "76 Trombones." This year, the perennial crowd pleaser presented country singer Martina McBride performing "Happy Girl." For the youngsters, *Sesame Street* characters, who were celebrating their 30th television season, rode aboard the Friends for Life float, singing their classic song, "Sing." Barney the Purple Dinosaur rode on his Gingerbread House float. The Soaring Spirit canoe float featured Judy Collins, who performed "The Fallow Way," and on Peter Pan's Pirate Ship float, Cathy Rigby, who was starring in Broadway's *Peter Pan,* sang "I've Gotta Crow." Making a return appearance was the Westward Ho! float; this covered wagon kept singer Jo Dee Messina dry as she sang "I'm Alright." Kenny Rogers, making his second parade appearance, escorted the Toms River, New Jersey, 1998 Little League World Champions, who had won the hearts of the nation, on the Statue of Liberty float. Rogers fittingly performed the song "Heroes."

Additional entertainment value was added by teen favorites, including 98 Degrees performing "Because of You" aboard the Mr. Peanut's Circus float, N'Sync performing their chart-busting hit "Tearin' Up My Heart" aboard the M&M Studios falloon, and Monica performing "Angel of Mine" on the Party Time float. Rounding out the lineup were the Pointer Sisters on the fantastic Rudolph the Red-Nosed Reindeer falloon. Veteran musicians Chicago, taking the S-Train (the Santaland Express float), performed a jazzy, show-stopping rendition of the holiday classic "Let It Snow!" Country singer Kevin Sharp rode the Annabelle's Wish float, and the New York Yankees, represented by Manager Joe Torre, David Cone, and Orlando "El Duque" Hernandez, traveled the route atop the Big Apple float.

Unfortunately, Spiderman, Garfield, and the Quik bunny had developed leaks during the night and were taken out of the lineup. The Wild Thing, which had missed its test flight, could not get past the starting line because he sustained an injury after being raised into the air above his inflation tarp. After two-and-a-half hours of rain, Santa arrived in Herald Square under clear skies, providing the perfect ending.

On Saturday, November 13, 1999, the weather turned out to be perfect for balloon test flights before the 73rd edition of the parade. The three new balloons exhibited just the right touch of Macy's magic. Millennium Snoopy, who donned a court jester's hat and held a party horn labeled "Macy's 2000," became the Macy's mascot for the upcoming holiday season.

In a wonderful nod both to Macy's mechanical windows, which were phased out in the 1960s, and to the 1947 film *Miracle on 34th Street,* Maureen O'Hara appeared at the Herald Square store the week before the parade and oversaw the unveiling of the Christmas windows. In the film, O'Hara played Doris Walker, the woman in charge of the parade. O'Hara recalled memories of the film, remarking, "I know John Payne, Natalie Wood, and Kris Kringle [Edmund Gwenn] are up in heaven looking down on us and smiling." Anticipation was high that year. Would the parade meet and exceed everyone's expectations?

Thanksgiving week's weather was murky, and morning showers were in the forecast. On Inflation Eve—as the night before the parade, when the balloons are inflated, has become known—the weather was gorgeous, unseasonably warm, and free from rain, allowing for a record turnout. On Thanksgiving, November 25, 1999, just before the start of the parade, the rain showers grew in intensity. Despite the weather, a repeat of the year before, crowd estimates were at two million. New Yorkers are a tough bunch, as are the tourists.

Promptly at 9:00 a.m., the NBC television cameras focused on *Today Show* hosts Katie Couric and Matt Lauer for the introduction of weatherman Al Roker and Macy's Jean McFaddin, Joseph Denofrio, and Craig Miller uptown at 77th Street. "Five, four, three, two, one, let's have a parade," McFaddin and all proclaimed. America Sings! set the tone of the parade with a rendition of "Heading for the Future." Spectators were treated to some of Broadway's finest shows. The cast of *Saturday Night Fever,* newly opened on Broadway, provided the number "Night Fever," and the cast of *Fosse* performed "Bye, Bye, Blackbird." After the traditional appearance from the Radio City Rockettes, who performed the outstanding "A Marshmallow World," the lively show *Swing* was represented by a jumping and swinging performance, clearing the way for the critically hailed revival of *Kiss Me Kate* and the song "Another Opening." In a blizzard of confetti, the 73rd annual Macy's Thanksgiving Day Parade was ready to march in front of the crowds at Macy's, with Cloe the Clown flying high. The balloon is hailed as the guardian spirit of the clowns and is an important part of the parade. As Jean McFaddin and other parade officials waved to the crowds, NBC broadcaster Matt Lauer mentioned that McFaddin had received the honor of being inducted into the International Festival and Events Association Hall of Fame.

The Virgil Grissom High School Marching Band of Huntsville, Alabama, started the procession with a rousing rendition of "A Brand New Day." The Soaring Spirit canoe float, with the students of the American Indian College Fund aboard, brought to mind American Indians and their role in the first Thanksgiving. Tom Turkey had the honor of escorting Susan Lucci, a daytime television star and ambassador for a Hunger-Free Holiday. The usual appearance of the Sesame Street float, Muppets, and cast did not disappoint as they performed "How Do You Do?" The Medieval Times float featured two smoke-spewing dragons, and Ask Jeeves, a new icon from the Internet who appeared in float form, gave Miss America Heather French the perfect stage to perform "Why Do Fools Fall in Love?" The U.S. Mint debuted a new coin, to be issued in 2000, on its Golden Dollar Stagecoach float, which featured country singing act SheDaisy performing "Little Goodbyes."

On the Statue of Liberty float, the Bacon brothers, Kevin and Michael, performed "Don't Look Back." The Animal Planet float featured Terri Irwin from *Crocodile Hunter.* Along for the ride was Broadway star Jeremy Kushnier, who sang "Crocodile Rock" as a huge croc snapped in time. One of the most stirring numbers in the parade was Lillias White's rendition of "Just Beyond the Dream," performed with the U.S. Naval Academy Men's Glee Club. The song, cowritten by Macy's own William Schermerhorn, ended in a display of sparklers and rockets to mark it as the theme song for Macy's 2000 Fireworks and Op/Sail 2000. Although only 13 years old, Charlotte Church sang a beautiful, powerful "Just Wave Hello" on the Millennium Time Continuum float. Holiday spirit was provided by Barney the Purple Dinosaur on Barney's Night before Christmas, a richly detailed float with a toy train.

On the Rudolph the Red-Nosed Reindeer falloon, Florence Henderson of *The Brady Bunch* sang the popular reindeer song. Getting the party started, Lou Bega performed his catchy "Mambo No. 5," while the new Captain Kangaroo, John McDonough, mamboed along on the Caribbean Fiesta falloon. Christina Aguilera took a trip on the M&M's Network falloon, singing "What a Girl Wants." The rhythm-and-blues group Kool and the Gang set the tone with "Millenium Celebration," an updated version of their famous song "Celebration," on the Jello-Bration falloon. Keeping the music moving were a total of 11 marching bands from locales such as California, Texas, Ohio, Louisiana, Georgia, Wisconsin, and even Petticoat Junction, South Carolina.

Despite the rain during the three-hour telecast, the balloons enjoyed nearly perfect flying weather. Garfield was the senior balloon, making his 16th appearance. The Rocky and Bullwinkle balloon made its second parade appearance. Macy's Harold the Fireman balloon, the flying fish, and Petula the Pig also joined the roster. This year was Petula the Pig's first trip down to Macy's. The giant balloons were escorted by 19 novelty balloons.

Upon the arrival of the Macy's Santaland Express and Coal Car—a magical re-creation of a steam locomotive engine bedecked with holiday garland and poinsettias—the crowd was treated to a performance of the new holiday song "This Gift" by 98 Degrees. The engine billowed smoke high into the air above Herald Square, and the engine's whistle prepared the way for Santa Claus. The Comeaux High Marching Band of Lafayette, Louisiana, played "Santa Claus is Coming to Town," having the honor of heralding Santa's spectacular arrival and the end of the 73rd parade.

Once again, colorful advertisements trumpeted the parade's arrival in 2000. Wednesday night, November 22, was brutally cold. Despite the frigid chill, Inflation Eve brought out the largest number of spectators in recent memory. The NBC telecast started with Al Roker presenting Jean McFaddin with a pair of golden scissors and Manfred G. Bass with a golden hammer for their years of dedicated parade work. The gesture set the tone for the parade ahead, celebrating the work and dedication of the entire Macy's family. The forecast for Thanksgiving Day offered a frigid air mass but, thankfully, no rain.

The telecast began with the traditional appearance of America Sings! performing "Believe in Music," followed by performances from Broadway's *The Music Man,* the new musical *Seussical,* and

Cheryl Ladd performing music from the hit revival of *Annie Get Your Gun*. The crowd saw the Rockettes ready to take to the streets of old New York and perform a medley of "Strike Up the Band" and "Alexander's Ragtime Band."

The police motorcycle brigade had the honor of escorting Macy's Joseph Denofrio, Craig Miller, and Jean McFaddin. The first band that came into view was the Lincoln High School Marching Band of Sioux Falls, South Dakota, playing "Strike Up the Band." Tom Turkey followed with the Corrs, who performed "Breathless," one of the best openings in the parade's broadcast history. From the Jello World of Wiggle float, Jo Dee Messina sang "Dare to Dream." LFO sang "West Side Story" from the Rip Van Winkle float. New teen favorite BBMak sang a new song called "Still On My Side." The girl group Innosence performed "Say No More." For the younger set, there was Aaron Carter, the little brother of the Backstreet Boys' Nick Carter, who sang "I Want Candy." The float that carried him down the city streets was Simple Simon's Fair. For just the right touch of nostalgia, the former child star of *Annie*, Andrea McArdle, a Macy's Thanksgiving Day Parade veteran, greeted the crowds from the Rudolph the Red-Nosed Reindeer falloon. Standing alongside her was her daughter. Once the parade had passed, officials and staff gathered to toast Jean McFaddin, who had guided the parade through 25 years. Under her leadership, the parade became a spectacular high-stepping treat for all ages.

A few questions were recently answered by two of the main figures behind the parade: when do the parade team members celebrate Thanksgiving, and do they ever feel melancholy that the parade is over? McFaddin responded, "On the Friday after Thanksgiving, Macy's provides a wonderful dinner out at the Parade Studio, which all of the parade production team bring their families to. It's a wonderful event, but I confess I always get a little melancholy when I look at all the faces gathered at one giant table. I know how much effort everybody put into creating that year's parade—how much love we have for it—and, suddenly, it's another sweet memory." With a wonderful spark in his eye, Manfred Bass continued, "But we're already dreaming what we're going to do next year! We gotta have this; we gotta do that. And we say we can't believe we're talking about next year." McFaddin agreed, "Everybody gets excited all over again."

Bass reflected on what is it like on the big day, after weeks of working on the parade. "Leading up to the parade, you never realize the various levels—the full dimensions—of the parade unless you're personally involved. It's so amazing. You work all year, and then it comes down to those last few hours before it steps off on Thanksgiving morning. For those of us up at 77th Street, the magic hour is really between 5:00 and 6:00 a.m. You just begin to see the sun quietly coming up over the trees in Central Park, and suddenly, bam! The entire mood changes. By 7:00 a.m., the buses just start pouring and pouring in, unloading thousands of clowns, float escorts, and marching bands. We've been working all night preparing the balloons and assembling the floats and now, in the glow of that glorious dawn, the thousands and thousands of parade marchers bring it all to life. It's bright. It's colorful."

"It's showtime!" McFaddin chimed in. Bass continued, "Suddenly, there is real electricity in the air because everybody is so excited. It doesn't matter if there's a faint drizzle in the air. It doesn't matter if there's a little snowflake coming down to dance with the rest of us. There's a magical warmth in that exciting moment. The balloons are set; the people are ready to go. And then, you hear a whistle—'Let's have a parade!'" After 78 years of parades, it is still a thrill to see. May it go on for another 78 years, and another. Let's have a parade!

The 1994 parade introduced two new balloon characters: Barney, 59 feet tall and a hit with the younger set, and Dr. Seuss's the Cat in the Hat. Television cameras in Herald Square beamed pre-parade performances from the shows *Beauty and the Beast, Grease, Damn Yankees,* and *Showboat* to home viewers before the parade reached Macy's. (Courtesy of Macy's.)

SIDE ELEVATION

SCALE 1 : 1.00

One of the most gloriously rich and detailed floats was the Indian Canoe float, seen in this 1986 drawing. It is the perfect example of the level of artistry that goes into taking a float from design to completion. (Courtesy of Macy's. Illustration by Manfred Bass.)

The Quik bunny, seen here in 1995, has become a classic balloon. (Photograph by Bill Smith.)

In 1987, Spiderman, a favorite comic book character, came to life in a magnificent balloon that was a crowd pleaser for many parades. The balloon is seen here in 1995. Spidey was fitted with a camera to give viewers a balloon's-eye perspective of the streets. He also had the distinction of being the second balloon to travel to England (the first being Kermit the Frog). (Photograph by Bill Smith.)

In 1997, the real thing was in sight: the parade had reached Herald Square. What followed were two more hours of attractions, including Shari Lewis with her wooly friend Lamb Chop on the parade mainstay, the Turkey float. Santa had a little helper, it seemed, as Lamb Chop looked the part, dressed as jolly St. Nick. (Courtesy of Macy's.)

Besides the Indian Canoe float, the country contingent in 1997 was represented by superstars Tim McGraw, riding a covered wagon pulled by a giant mechanical bull, and Randy Travis and Beth Nielsen Chapman, riding on the Annabelle's Wish float. (Courtesy of Macy's.)

From balloon to falloon, Humpty Dumpty, pictured here in 1994, is pure Macy's magic. (Courtesy of Macy's.)

In 1994, in addition to the appearance of highflying Garfield, perennial parade favorites from *Sesame Street* performed their hit "Rubber Ducky" to the delight of youngsters everywhere. Deborah Gibson hoped to "shake your love" as she performed "Only in My Dreams" on the M&M's Chocolate Colorworks falloon. (Courtesy of Macy's.)

Blue (right), the blue dog from *Blue's Clues*, was the ninth female character balloon in the parade's history, debuting in 1999. The Honey-Nut Cheerios Bee (center), a popular cereal star for 20 years, and Millennium Snoopy also made their debuts on Broadway in 1999. There have been four balloon incarnations of Snoopy, the most of any character to date. (Photograph by Christopher Hoskins.)

Inflation Eve received coverage in all the major newspapers and on all the television stations in 1998. The balloons were all being given their recommended yearly dose of vitamin H—helium, that is. The evening was perfect for the large crowds jamming 77th and 81st Streets along Central Park West. With only 12 hours until parade time, the excitement was building. (Photograph by Christopher Hoskins.)

In 2002, Clifford the Big Red Dog looks fetching under the net on 81st Street. (Photograph by Christopher Hoskins.)

In 2000, at the Meadowlands in New Jersey, Macy's presented to the media four new balloon superstars who were to join the veteran parade balloons in the rapidly approaching 74th annual Macy's Thanksgiving Day Parade. The day was picture perfect, with temperatures in the mid- to upper 50s. With the press corps ready for photo opportunities, bandleader Mickey Mouse took to the skies. Next, Ronald McDonald easily made his test flight. Jeeves, from AskJeeves.com, was asked the question "Are you ready for your flight?" The answer was yes! Cassie from *Dragon Tales* made the trip last. The new balloons were a big hit, and all was in readiness for the big parade. (Photograph by Christopher Hoskins.)

In the 2000 parade, every balloon traveled the route in fine fashion and was greeted as a returning hero. Bandleader Mickey Mouse made a triumphant debut, as did other newcomers Ronald McDonald, Jeeves, and Cassie. A re-creation of the 1940s Gnome balloon, now christened the Macy's Elf, also flew. The one mishap was that Rocky could not ride piggyback on his pal Bullwinkle; Rocky had deflated the night before. (Photograph by Christopher Hoskins.)

The 75th anniversary parade advertisement from 2001 captured all the magic of the parade. (Courtesy of Macy's.)

# Nine

# PRESENT DAY

## THE PARADE

## UPLIFTS THE NATION

September 11, 2001, dawned bright and sunny. Then, before 9:00 a.m., the nation was shaken to its very core as terrorists struck New York's World Trade Center and the Pentagon in Washington, D.C. The next few months were a time of national mourning. In trying to make sense of the tragedy, Americans discovered that the best way to carry on was to do simply that—carry on. As in 1963, when John F. Kennedy was assassinated less than one week before the parade, Macy's found itself faced with a tough decision. Again, the decision was that the parade would go on.

On November 22, 2001, Robin Hall, Macy's new parade producer, and his team put on a parade that unified the country. Parade participants marched, remembering and honoring the people who had lost their lives two months earlier. They showed the world that America would not be afraid to celebrate the freedom for which so many had died. Tom Turkey graciously gave up his usual first position to the Statue of Liberty float, and Broadway's Betty Buckley sang "America, the Beautiful" in Herald Square.

America Sings! kicked off the telecast after an introduction by hosts Katie Couric and Matt Lauer and guest Mayor Rudolph Giuliani. Broadway was represented by the shows *Mama Mia, 42nd Street, Thou Shalt Not,* and a knockout performance by the cast of *Contact.*

The new balloon stars on the block were Curious George (also celebrating his 60th birthday), Nickelodeon's Jimmy Neutron, a newly designed Big Bird, *Pokemon's* Pikachu, and Cheesasaurus Rex. All flew proudly in the patriotic air of the day.

Pop star Usher sang "You Remind Me" on the M&M's Network falloon. Parade returnee singer Charlotte Church, at 15 years old, graced the Mother Earth float with her glorious voice. Top talent continued with Boys II Men and country's Billy Ray Cyrus singing a rousing "We the People" atop the Spirit of America float.

As the year also marked the parade's 75th anniversary, Macy's presented veteran employees and parade volunteers on a vintage Macy's REO truck. One rider on the truck was a balloon handler in the 1927 parade. The Parade of Parades float included past parade favorites, such as Popeye, Olive Oyl, and Underdog, all waving to the crowds.

Bands, bands, and more bands—from Montana, Texas, and Hawaii—marched in musical step. Once Santa appeared in Herald Square, the parade ended and work began for the following year's parade. For some three hours, all had seemed right in the world.

November 28, 2002, marked the 76th parade. With thermometers frozen at 27 degrees at parade time, hosts Katie Couric and Matt Lauer joined America Sings! in Herald Square at the start of the telecast. The 850 voices that make up the group got the street party under way. Star Patty Duke headlined the performance of Broadway's *Oklahoma,* and *Thoroughly Modern Millie* thoroughly entertained, as did performances from *The Producers* and *Hairspray.*

Uptown, Al Roker interviewed Kermit the Frog and Miss Piggy in honor of a newly designed Kermit balloon. Tom Turkey happily returned to his position leading the way for the new balloon stars, such as Little Bill, Charlie Brown and the Elusive Football, Mr. Monopoly, and Macy's re-creation of the 1939 Uncle Sam balloon. Returning favorites included Ronald McDonald, Big Bird, and Jimmy Neutron.

Down on earth, star power included Lee Ann Womack on the Dinotopia float, Ashanti on the M&M's Network falloon, *American Idol* runner-up Justin Guarini, and the Wiggles, the Australian favorite of the very young set, on the Jolly Polly pirate ship.

Bands, all standouts, included first-time parade performers Piscataway High School of Piscataway, New Jersey; Salem High School of Salem, North Carolina; and Prospect High School of Mount Prospect, Illinois. And the always-in-step Radio City Rockettes made the crowd cheer, as did the arrival of Santa Claus.

The statistics on the 77th parade, held on November 27, 2003, were spectacular. More than 12,000 people marched in the parade—a Macy's record—and three million people lined the route. The weather provided temperatures in the mid-40s, and the sights were truly memorable.

The four Broadway shows getting prime parade attention were *Never Gonna Dance, Wicked, Little Shop of Horrors,* and *The Boy from Oz*. Balloons were high in the sky, with Garfield celebrating his 25th birthday in grand style in his second balloon incarnation. The Strike Up the Band Barney balloon struck the right chord. *Sesame Street's* Super Grover—yes, a super balloon—followed the Gorgeous Gobbler, a Macy's re-creation of the vintage balloon. For the first time, Tom Turkey took a holiday.

The marching bands from Jones High School of Orlando, Florida, Roosevelt High School of Honolulu, Hawaii, and Franklin Regional High School of Murrysville, Pennsylvania, were just a few that kept the march moving amongst grand floats, returning balloon favorites (Arthur the Aardvark marked his sixth parade appearance), and celebrities.

Singer Stacie Orrico entertained crowds from the Green Dog falloon, and Ruben Studdard, the *American Idol* winner, wooed the crowds from Hess's Bridge to the Future. *American Idol* runner-up Clay Aiken sang from the Hershey Kids Candy Creation Lab. Pop superstars and parade veterans Kool and the Gang sang "Jungle Boogie" on the Animal Planet float. The pop group Chicago made its second parade appearance, performing "Jolly Ol' St. Nick" on the Marion Carol Showboat. Hillary Duff, aboard the American Classic Malt Shop float, sang, so appropriately, "So Yesterday."

Happily, once again, the Radio City Rockettes and the cast of *Sesame Street* celebrated Santa's arrival.

This 2003 advertisement is a feast for the eyes. (Courtesy of Macy's.)

Kermit is a balloon for the second time in 2003. (Photograph by Bill Smith.)

Charlie Brown became a truly spectacular parade balloon in 2002. (Photograph by Christopher Hoskins.)

Not yet a parade star but soon to be, Dino is pictured in Akron, Ohio, in 1963. (Courtesy of Goodyear Tire and Rubber Company collection, University of Akron Archives.)

The parade took on a new glow beginning in 1977, the year Jean McFaddin took the helm. This native Texan had a background in theater and a deep love for New York, and she adored the excitement that both offered. A lifelong fan of the parade since watching the first national telecast as a child in Texas, she realized that in order for it to grow, the parade needed to have a larger, yearlong department. She built on the existing team, bringing together even more talented people and top-notch artists. Creativity soared, and new balloon superstars took flight. More floats were added, as were more clowns and more Broadway shows. Throughout her 24-year career at Macy's, she expressed her belief that the parade is the world's most wonderful stage. As a result, this talented producer presented a wealth of joyful entertainment that celebrates Macy's, New York City, and America. In a lasting show of her talent, she built a bigger and better parade—a parade that continues to shine as brightly as the Macy's trademark star balloons that fly high above the streets of New York City in every Macy's Thanksgiving Day Parade.

Robin Hall was the maker of Macy's Magic 2001 Thanksgiving Day parade. Sharing his predecessor's love of the theater and passion for New York City, Hall expressed his great respect for the work that has made the parade what it is and vowed to make the parade bigger and better every year. His first production marked the parade's 75th anniversary. That formidable challenge was magnified by the tragic events of September 11, 2001. Hall and his team put on what may be one of the most important parades in recent history—a parade received gratefully by New York City and America to balance the somber mood that had engulfed the country in the aftermath of the terrorist attacks. Record crowds lined the streets to witness the enduring pageant of the Macy's Thanksgiving Day Parade, which this time featured tributes to the heroes of September 11. Since 2001, the parade has continued to grow and flourish. Elements not seen in the parade in 50 years have returned, and new elements never seen in any parade have been added. New ideas constantly are being tested for the future, assuring that the parade will continue to grow bigger and better.

The second Superman balloon in the parade's history appears in this stunning color shot at its test flight in 1966. (Courtesy of Goodyear Tire and Rubber Company collection, University of Akron Archives.)